Morgantown to S

Julian Martin

Also from Julian Martin

Imagonna: Peace Corps Memories

The Soviet Union and Lincoln County USA

Sarvice Mountain *(a novel)*

Cruising the Acropolis

Damn Yankee Buttons

Secular Mann *(Perry Mann essays)*

Vietnam Dope *(As told to Julian Martin)*

Chapters

W L
Yosemite
Taxi
The Zodiac Killer
Finocchios
Murder at the Cab Station
Gone Postal
Lawrence Hall of Science
Emeryville
Hare Krishna
god-Man Two
Home Court
CRV Committee of Returned Volunteers
Cuba
Defending America Against an Internal Enemy
Random Sightings
The Carson Street Players
Sandy Weinstein
Barbara Herzig
Glide Memorial Methodist Church
Home Again
Hell's Angels
Crowe Farm
Feelings of Murder
Don's Orphanage
Vancouver
Get in Friend
Technocracy
Winnipeg

My Back Room
Country Roads
Chicago and Home

Morgantown

Mike Breiding remembers:

For us, at least for me, moving to Morgantown was like moving to New York City. It was the 60s and we were Morgantown's only hippie family.

My mom was a radical by the standards of the day what with taking her kids to Peace Marches in Washington DC and New York City to protest the war in Vietnam and throwing parties for WVU International Students from around the globe.

After years of social isolation she was ready to enjoy herself. One of the things mom did to make this happen was stop in one day at the Foreign Student Office, where she met WVU Foreign Student Advisor Julian Martin. And before you know it mom had signed up to act as a host family for foreign students attending WVU.

Anyway, the upshot is that all of a sudden mom and all us six kids were socializing with young college students from all over the world. In 1960's Morgantown this was unheard of. People would openly stare when they saw an African walking down the main street of downtown.

As you can imagine, meeting someone from Kenya or Thailand or Persia was exciting and fun for all of us. And my sisters? They were two gorgeous teens who were the center of attention at every party or get together.

Mom was different and she wanted to stay that way. But this could not happen while married to someone whose mantra was "Don't question authority," while my mom's was always "Question Authority".

So, it was time to leave all that behind in search of a life which would allow her and her children to express themselves and think as they wished. And where else but San Francisco could that dream be realized.

Poison Hemlock

Samuel P. Taylor State Park in Marin County, is about a thirty to forty-five-minute drive north of The City[1]. The park is not too far from the city of Fairfax. Gene, our Free School teacher, had decided it would be educational to take the four of us on a trip over to Marin County and explore the woods there. We parked at the gate for the access road for Kent Lake, a reservoir which supplies drinking water to Marin County. The woods were lush and thick with small tributaries feeding into the main stem of the creek from the lake.

At some point, we came across a plant that we all knew from home. We told Gene it was in the carrot family and it had a sweet tasting, carrot-like root, which we had eaten before. The plants we had found here at the Park were much larger than the plants we had back home West Virginia. We attributed that to the fact they were growing in Californian, why, I don't know.

We wrestled several of the plants out of the ground and began munching away on the

---

[1] *"The City" is San Francisco*

11

sweet, tasty roots. We all had some, except Gene. Shortly after that we all piled back into Gene's 1968 Camaro, which I thought was a really cool car, and started the drive back to San Fran. At some point I told Gene I was feeling sick and felt sure I was going to throw up. Gene found a gas station and I got out of the car and headed to the bathroom. I never made it. I fell to the ground and became convulsively ill. The last thing I remember was literally being thrown into an ambulance.

I am now unsure of the timeline, but around two days later I regained consciousness. As my eyes focused and I became somewhat aware of my surroundings, I felt a sharp pain "down there." My hand went to my privates, and to my horror, I found there was some sort of tube going up inside of me. At that point in my life, I had never heard of a catheter.

I looked around and to my left there was a glass room. Inside of it, was my brother Wayne lying in bed. This was a bizarre scene and it frightened me. I was to find out later this was an isolation unit he had been put in because he had contracted a staph infection.

At some point a nurse came by and of course I uttered the usual question: "Where am I?" She told me we were in the hospital. She said the plant we had eaten had poisoned us and we had been made quite sick. Quite sick, meant being in a coma for two days and nearly dying.

Apparently, when we got to the hospital no one was sure what to do. As I understand it, Gene told them about the plant we had eaten, which was the suspected culprit for the nasty turn of events. I think at that point, Gene went back to the site with a botanist who collected and identified the plant as poison hemlock, which was known to be quite toxic—a piece of root the size of a walnut has been known to kill a cow, and a single root has been known to kill a horse.

But even with this information the required treatment was not known. The toxic alkaloid had to be isolated and identified and then a treatment regimen devised to try to save us. The end result of this were complete transfusions, for my brother Wayne and me, and being continuously medicated with Dilantin and phenobarbital. It was thought the transfusions would clear the toxin from our systems and the drugs would control the violent convulsions we had been experiencing. The big fear was brain damage. So, to this day I have had a handy excuse for every stupid thing I have done.

"Four Brothers Stricken Down" was picked up by the wire services and reported in the national press. People who know us personally read about it and some assumed the story ended in tragedy or heard no more about it. So, imagine my surprise, when, the first time I go back to visit Morgantown, after a four-year absence, I find out a number of people thought I was dead."

November 22, 1963

Several time zones away it was late night on board a Russian ship heading for the Bosphorus Strait and Istanbul. The ship's bartender turned the radio up so that I and the other two men in the bar, both also Americans, could hear it better.

Four semesters of Russian language courses, six years before at West Virginia University, weren't a lot of help. I made out Kennedy and Lee Harvey Oswald's names, and Dallas, Texas. One of the other men in the bar said that Kennedy *was* supposed to be in Dallas that day.

I went back to our cabin and woke my wife Joyce, to tell her the shocking news. We talked all night. We tried to comprehend that the man whose call we had answered to teach in Africa for the past two years, had been murdered. Our president had been murdered!

The next day a young Russian woman said, with a taunting voice, "Yes! Kennedy is dead." I looked angrily at her and she tried to apologize with, "Oh! I am sorry." She said, and I replied, "You sure are sorry." Her reaction was opposite to what we saw in our Moscow hotel a few days later—the maids were weeping as they watched Kennedy's funeral on television.

On our way from Piraeus to Odessa, our ship made a four-hour stop in Istanbul. We bought a newspaper. A taxi driver took us to a University area where we found students who interpreted the newspaper story of Kennedy's death. One of the students expressed joy that Kennedy had been killed. In anger, I walked away, saying, "I have had enough of Turks." Just a year after that, as the Foreign Student Advisor at West Virginia University, I was friends with some students from Turkey. They invited me to sit with them in a restaurant and added in jest, "If you don't mind sitting with Turks." A prejudice felt.

My world accelerated its ugly slide into intolerance, accompanied with violence. In September 1963, just two months before our Peace Corps experience in Nigeria ended, Klu Klux Klan terrorists bombed the 26th Street Baptist Church in Birmingham, Alabama. Four Sunday school girls were killed, another girl's eye was put out, and over twenty other people were injured. My African students were puzzled, "How could that happen in America."

As I write this the voters of Alabama just elected Doug Jones to the United States Senate. Nearly forty years after the murders and destruction at the Birmingham church, Doug Jones had been the lead prosecutor in the successful prosecution of two of the Klan bigots who bombed the church.

With 98% of the female African-American votes, Democrat Jones defeated Republican, racist, pedophile, Roy Moore. Enough Alabama Republicans, maybe not bothered as much by his racism, could not vote for a pedophile.[2]

On our way home from two years in the Peace Corps, my wife and I encountered a feeling of wonder and respect everywhere we went. It was innocence like the Puerto Rican girls in West Side Story singing, "I like to be in America! O.K. by me in America! Everything free in America! For a small fee in America!" That good feeling was before Selma, Birmingham, burned Freedom Rider buses, three bodies under a dam in Mississippi, the Vietnam War, the murders of Medgar Evers, Martin Luther King, Jr., Robert Kennedy, and the beating of African Americans sitting peacefully at

---

[2]*www.al.com/news/index.ssf/2017/12/how_did_doug_jones_win_wo men_a.html*

lunch counters and police using dogs and water hoses against African-American protestors. Memories of the torture and murder of Emmett Till in 1955, remind that African-Americans have been brutalized since they were "freed" by the Civil War.

Student Days 1954-59

Curtis (Hank) Barnett, who would later become CEO of Bethlehem Steel, invited me to a Beta Theta Pi fraternity picnic at Lower Falls Beach on Big Coal River and sponsored me as a pledge prospect at West Virginia University. Through that process I met: Chuck Haden, who would become a Federal Judge, and rule against coal companies on mountain top removal strip mining for coal; Roger Tomkins, who spearheaded nullifying the death penalty in West Virginia; and Tom McHugh, like his friend Chuck Haden, a future West Virginia Supreme Court Justice.

When I arrived at West Virginia University my hair was long. I had a six-day-a-week August job. For one dollar an hour I sprayed herbicide on telephone and electric powerline rights-of-way. I had no time for a haircut.

That herbicide was an auxin[3] that composed 50% of agent orange used to defoliate forests in the Vietnam war. It caused extremely rapid cell division and uncontrollable plant growth. The

---

[3] *A class of plant hormones*

barrels of the concentrated auxin were labeled 2,4 D.

I remember that a young man climbed on top of a Dodge Power Wagon's 500-gallon tank, filled it with water and added one gallon of the 2,4 D. We sprayed that five hundred to one diluted solution on the plant growth in the rights-of-way—it caused plants to grow so fast that tree bark couldn't keep up and was busted, and in two days the trees were dead.[4]

For one month, I went home from work every day with my clothes soaked in 2,4 D solution—we teenagers sometimes had battles with the streams from the high-pressure hoses that could shoot a hundred feet. Agent Orange—which is 50% 2,4 D—is capable of damaging genes, resulting in deformities among the offspring of exposed victims. The U.S. government has documented higher cases of leukemia, Hodgkin's lymphoma, and various kinds of cancer in exposed veterans.[5]

So far, at 82, I don't have symptoms or any of the diseases known to be caused by exposure[6] to 2,4,D.

---

[4] *www.toxipedia.org/display/toxipedia/2%2C4-D*
[5] *Wikipedia*
[6] *https://www.nrdc.org/stories/24-d-most-dangerous-pesticide-*

I combed my long hair in a DA.[7] That hair style was not acceptable in a Beta Theta Pi prospect—when I realized that, I immediately ran my hand through the DA.

I was so innocent of the expectations of the Beta Theta Pi members that I wore a pink dress shirt to a pledge party. A Beta Theta Pi member said about my pink shirt, "We don't see many of those up here." Pink shirts, DA's, and rock and roll were part of high school culture but had not caught on in the fraternity circles. That did change.

An all-American football player of Greek heritage was a Beta Theta Pi member. During a discussion of the prospective pledges, it was said about one of the prospects, as a reason for his rejection, "He is a Greek." The football player said, "So, what's wrong with Greeks." Fraternities had Greek names and were referred to as Greeks. The irony of fraternity prejudice—no Greeks among the Greeks! Jews and African-Americans need not apply.

---

youve-never-heard
[7] *DA stands for Duck's Ass*

I was not prepared for college level work. The first semester was brutal, I managed to squeeze by with a 2.0 average. Without my genius room-mate Paul Davis, I would not have made it. He could do our math homework in half the time it took me. Paul was the first of two room-mates who, after graduating from West Virginia University, went to M.I.T.

Paul and I were disciplined—every evening we locked our door and studied for two hours and then took a short break and shot the bull with our dormitory neighbors. In our fourth year at West Virginia University, we were both elected to the student legislature as engineering school representatives.

Ralph Rippey was my room-mate after Paul Davis. Ralph was a veteran of four years in the Navy and was going to school on the G.I. Bill of Rights. Every morning, no matter how cold it was, he reached in the shower, turned the cold full blast and stepped in. Ralph walked at a fast pace, I almost had to run to keep up with him.

Ralph's father was killed in a railroad accident, causing his mother to have to work as a waitress to support her family. He remembered

Tucker County, West Virginia, with snow on his bed that came through cracks in the walls. Ralph is one of an amazing group of exceptional people I have met over the years—talented, compassionate, disciplined, and dedicated to doing what is right.

I argued with Joe Nay, my roommate after Ralph Rippey graduated, that Democrats force Republicans to be Christians. Joe's dad was a wildcat gas well driller and I figure very conservative in his politics, given that Joe sure was.

Joe came in dirty from a night shift at the bureau of mines and was shunned by the other students in an economics class he was required to take as part of engineering requirements. He was shunned, that is, until his 100 on the first test was passed down his aisle.

A couple of years later I visited Joe in Boston, where he was attending M.I.T. He had a calculus test coming up the next day. Joe started to look at the book to study. I asked his wife if he had studied before that—she said he hadn't opened the book. The next day, Joe got ninety percent on his first M.I.T. calculus test.

Joe Nay's brother Floyd[8], was also brilliant. In high school, he wrote a paper about plasma, not about blood plasma but about a plasma of charged particles[9]—I had never heard of it. After his freshman year at West Virginia University, he was appointed to the Air Force Academy where he tutored his classmates in the class or 1963. A classmate said, "…Floyd was flat-out too smart for the Academy…many benefited by Floyd devoting free time to tutoring and "dumbing down" various math and engineering concepts to a level where those struggling could get through and graduate. Floyd became an Air Commando and flew a *puff the magic dragon* gunship in Vietnam—its three miniguns fired 2,000 rounds per minute in support of soldiers on the ground.[10]

[8] *Joe and Floyd Nay grew up in Pullman, West Virginia, and attended Harrisville High School.*
[9] *https://electronics.howstuffworks.com/plasma-display1.htm*
[10] *http://www.guns.com/2015/08/07/the-spookiest-story-in-vietnam-the-ac-47-gunship-12-photos/*

Wesley Foundation

Student days at West Virginia University were a major influence in my decision to volunteer for the Peace Corps. At West Virginia University I was active in Wesley Foundation, the Methodist student center.

Hunting through some old files I found a speech in which I hoped that students coming to Wesley Foundation...*would be the kind of radical that Christ was and lend sanity to our society.* I encouraged them to, *ask your fellow citizens if it is right to pollute our streams and air, if it is right to strip off the tops of mountains....if it is right to endanger the health of every living creature and plant by placing radioactive hazards in the atmosphere, or for one man to live in economic splendor while others starve?* And I asked them *to ponder on what Christ meant when he told the rich young ruler to sell all he had and give it to the poor.*

I served a term as President of Wesley Foundation and as president of the Methodist student fraternity, Sigma Theta Epsilon.

A carload of us took turns driving Joe Nay's old Oldsmobile from Morgantown to Norman, Oklahoma, for a national convention of Sigma Theta Epsilon at the University of Oklahoma.

After driving all night we stopped for breakfast in West Memphis, Arkansas. The waitress brought our orders, mine had a white blob beside the scrambled eggs and bacon. "What is that?" I asked her." She said, as if offended, "Why, grits!" I had never had grits. I don't think most people in West Virginia were familiar with deep south grits. We are often thought of as part of Dixie because the Mason-Dixon line is part of our border with Pennsylvania. However, the northern tip of West Virginia is farther north than the southern edge of New Jersey. Another geographic surprise is that Virginia extends farther west than West Virginia.

The St. Andrews Methodist Church in St. Albans, West Virginia, and Wesley Foundation at West Virginia University expanded my appreciation of human diversity. Out of all this, Albert Schweitzer became one of my heroes. In Nigeria I learned of Schweitzer's clay feet— something common in idols.

Albert Schweitzer: A Stupendous Anachronism

About Schweitzer, I wrote this in my book *Imagonna: Peace Corps Memories:*

Having noted in my Peace Corps application that Albert Schweitzer was one of my heroes, I was surprised to learn that, like all idols, he had feet of clay. The "Grand Doctor" and Headmaster[11] were both dedicated to being missionaries and in many ways served the objects of their mission. Unfortunately they were also disrespectful, condescending, and at times violent toward their clients.

Tai Solarin, a Nigerian educator and author, wrote of Albert Schweitzer in 1963 in the *Lagos Daily News:*

When you were told that fourteen Lambarene[12] medical students were being trained in France, you scoffed, "You cannot change their mentality."...You would go down in European history as a colossus, but in

---

[11] *The headmaster Irish priest at my Peace Corps assignment in Nigeria.*
[12] *Schweitzer's hospital was in Lambarene, Gabon.*

African history as a Robinson Crusoe who would rather have his man Friday always as a faithful dog. We would remember you as a friendly enemy and a stupendous anachronism.

After twenty-eight years in Africa, Schweitzer, who could speak several European languages, could not speak one African language.[13] The African genius for dealing with Europeans was frustrating and often infuriating for the good missionary, as it was for [my]Headmaster. The African manipulation of the system, by evasion and slow-motion reaction to orders, were to Europeans obvious character flaws. Africans were trying to survive in the new order of things and they invented their own ways.

The sainted Albert Schweitzer never trained nor hired one African doctor or nurse at his hospital in Gabon. He saw Africans as little children who must be cared for and protected by benevolent Europeans. Schweitzer wrote:

A word about the relations between the whites and the blacks. The Negro is a child, and with children, nothing can be done without the use of authority. We must,

[13] John Gunther, *Inside Africa* (New York, Harper, 1955).

therefore, so arrange the circumstances of daily life that my natural authority can find expression. With regard to the Negroes, then, I have coined the formula: "I am your brother, it is true, but your elder brother."[14]

Bill Shurtleff [15] wrote, in his *A Peace Corps Year with Nigerians,* about his visit to Lambarene, Gabon, where he worked for Schweitzer during a two-month break from a Nigerian Peace Corps assignment:

Dr. Schweitzer has been called one of the foremost prophets of our century. In him exists the Renaissance ideal of excellence in all things and a vigorous combination of the contemplation and the life of action. He is the unprecedented holder of four doctoral degrees in Theology, Philosophy, Music, and Medicine. His books, Quest of the Historical Jesus, The Philosophy of Civilization, and The Life of J. S. Bach, while only a part of his extensive writings, have made important contributions to Western thought. He is a world-famous organist and the winner of the Nobel Peace Prize in 1954. The size of his daily correspondence is absolutely

[14] John Gunther, Inside Africa *(New York, Harper, 1955).*

unbelievable, but he answers every letter personally, refusing to type or use a secretary. It has been suggested that his collected letters and writings might well make the most extensive literature ever produced by a single man. For a man of ninety, the doctor has the physical and mental energy of many men half his age. His hand is still as steady as when he was a young surgeon.

His eyes are unique, yet remind me vividly of Albert Einstein's in a picture by Joseph Karsh; large and full of wonder, almost childlike, seeming to be near laughter even when his face is stern or tired. Without preconceptions, I believe, one would sense great kindness and wisdom, and perhaps the iron-willed self-discipline of a man who is occasionally hard on others, always hard on himself.

The previously quoted praise of Schweitzer notwithstanding, Shurtleff had this to say about Schweitzer's feet of clay:

Dr. Schweitzer, like Saint Francis, has a love of animals which is so genuine as to almost seem strange to new visitors. This bond to, and communion with all things that live, is the essence of his philosophy of reverence for life, the central ethical principle in his writings...This love of animals gives rise to a true if not unfortunate story. An African was ill and one of the nurses felt it necessary to bring him extra food from the kitchen, but this she knew was not allowed. So she said that her dog was sick and got a great bowl of rice and meat with no questions asked. Nor is this an isolated or extraneous tale. Reverence for life seems all too often to be reverence for plants, animals, and Europeans, but somehow partially omits the Africans. How many of the truly dedicated nurses here are deeply bothered by this attitude on the part of those in charge of the hospital! It is a constant topic of private conversation in the evenings. For a hospital of 500 sick people there is not a single latrine or toilet. Incredible! Numerous nurses have urged the doctor to let them construct such a latrine in their spare time or at no extra cost, since the surrounding grounds, they assert, are full of disease from the excreta. But the doctor forbids this, saying that it is not necessary for the Africans. One nurse left the hospital recently because of this very issue.

...The floors are in many cases only irregular dirt, soiled by the goats, dogs, and chickens which are free to enter. The tuberculosis patients do not live in isolation, and whole families live in this building together. The floor, I am told, is damp when it rains, and water seeps in from the hillside. As one nurse sums up the situation: "The people come here with one disease and leave with two."

...His philosophy is to provide for the Gabonese a home away from home, which is neither much different nor much better than their normal living quarters in the forest, but which provides adequate medical service. The people seem to be quite happy with their accommodations and the common man loves Dr. Schweitzer and prefers his hospital to the free government hospital on the opposite bank of the river in Lambarene, although the government service is completely free, while manual work is required here, when possible, as payment for food and medicine.

[The government hospital across the river] *...has iron-spring beds compared to wood planks here, electric lights in most rooms, cement floors, clean white interiors,*

32

and toilets which are used and well kept. Yet the government hospital is only half full, while we are always crowded here.

The newer buildings here are nicer than the old ones, having wood floors and clean tin siding. Dr. Schweitzer is very proud that the simplicity and adequacy have been maintained, and that the people seem at peace when they are here.

Working with groups of Gabonese laborers, the doctor is often a harsh and impatient master. He sometimes strikes the men with his hand, following small mistakes, and has slapped women for leaving several sticks of their firewood on the road when our Jeep was going. He also shouts at the men and refers to them constantly in German as "Diese verdammten Affen" *(these damned apes). Yet these are the people to whom he has devoted his life and full concern. This contradiction is central. It bothers many of us that he would never think of treating any European as he treats them. When once a worker had been sharply reprimanded for a small mistake that was my fault, and I admitted my "guilt" to the doctor, he replied tersely, "A white man is never mistaken."*

...Virtually no education or preventive medicine takes place here, yet nurses say that some native women are unable to explain what causes constant pregnancies.

Only the medical equipment is truly modern.

...the doctor recalled his early days in Lambarene and the way that two Gabonese workers helped him to realize that a modern European hospital was not what the local people needed.

...Perhaps nowhere has the fullness of Lambarene been so well portrayed as in Norman Cousins' book: <u>Dr. Schweitzer of Lambarene.</u> Schweitzer, he concluded, must be judged not only for what he personally created, but for the great inspiration that his life has given to so many, since he has made his life his essential argument. He is as much a symbol as a fact. Aware of the criticisms...Mr. Cousins concludes that history will rightly count Dr. Schweitzer among her great men: "A man does not have to be an angel to be a saint."

Gandhi, My New Hero

William Minor, my philosophy professor at West Virginia University, rounded it all out. I came from his classes with Gandhi as one of my heroes. Years later I learned that Gandhi and I had the same birth date. Gandhi was murdered in 1948 when I was twelve years old and before I even heard of him. Too many of my heroes have been murdered.

About two months before I started learning to make Sidewinder missiles, I wrote in my journal:

Just this minute I have finished reading a work of spiritual and literary art. I have just finished a book by Kahlil Gibran called "The Prophet." This book ranks second only to the recorded words of Christ in spiritual wisdom.

Coal River

My first political action was a letter I wrote to the *Charleston Gazette,* protesting the condition of Coal River. I was in junior high school and few people in the working-class wrote letters to the editor—let alone a kid doing it. Coal River's banks were slick mud with a coat of black coal dust. Good enough, that's the name of the river isn't it? Well, it was Cole River at one time but that was probably just bad spelling.

Coal was first discovered in western Virginia, on what would become Big Coal River, at Peytona.

The next time I remember resisting the status quo was as a West Virginia University undergraduate in Monongalia county. But first, let me tell you how Monongalia county got its name.

Monongahela is said to be Native American for "river with falling banks." The Monongahela River flows through Monongalia County, north to Pittsburgh. It would have continued to the Saint Lawrence Seaway, but ice age glaciers left a pile of earth debris that dammed the river and eventually redirected it and the Allegheny River south, forming the Ohio River.

The Constitutional Convention of November 26, 1861, held to create West Virginia from Virginia, was held in Wheeling. The clerk of the convention asked for the spelling of that strange sounding county named for that strange river that flowed north. The delegates from the strange sounding county must have looked at one another suspecting that they all had a different version. Then as one man they may have deferred to their leader for his version. His version wasn't Monongahela County after the river but Monongalia County. Nobody was really sure how it was spelled. It must have been a hoot when they got home and found out they had misplaced Monongahela County forever and informed everyone that the place no longer existed.

Anyway, I became a little famous in our neighborhood for stepping out of the tight Appalachian formation and speaking my mind publicly about pollution of Coal River.

At West Virginia University, the Daily Athenaeum student newspaper carried an editorial that blasted Governor William Marland who was running for the United States Senate. The Governor was a drunk, probably driven there by the

Democratic legislators who acted like Republicans and destroyed his plan to put a severance tax on coal that was going out of West Virginia by the billions of tons and tax free.

I didn't vote for Marland for the Senate and I gave my grandpa a hard time for voting for a drunk. He said, "I would vote for a drunk Democrat before I would a Republican, any day." Now, I feel the same way.

The day after the editorial truth in the *Daily Athenaeum*, there was a line of black Cadillacs parked in front of the West Virginia University president's home. The truth business was going a bit too far. The Athenaeum editor was canned, and the faculty adviser resigned in protest. I confronted one of the reporters who said I was too idealistic that "idealism is idealism," I guess akin to, "it ain't over 'til it's over." The paper got back to reporting on panty raids and parking problems.

The editorial issue came up in political science class. The professor had been teaching about the importance of ethics in government and how noble many political philosophers were. I asked him about the censoring job the reagents had clamped on the Athenaeum—oops! The professor was active in Democratic politics in the county, so guess what. He had no trouble denouncing the editor for using the student newspaper for political purposes—I guess he figured it should have been a shopping guide. So much for truth in packaging for the professor.

Foreign Students

Betty Boyd, the Dean of Women and a mover and shaker at West Virginia University, wrote to me while I was in Africa. She was the West Virginia University Peace Corps liaison. I was the first West Virginia University and West Virginia Peace Corps volunteer.

Near the end of my Peace Corps experience, Miss Boyd's last letters were about the possibility of a job for me as Foreign Student Advisor at West Virginia University.

Miss Boyd was responsible for creating the position and hiring me as West Virginia University's first full-time foreign student advisor. She arranged for the University to buy a house and outfit it for foreign student advisor offices, a lounge, and living quarters for a few students. She named it International House.

There were 200 foreign students. Fifty were from East Africa in a US Agency for International Development agriculture education program. The African students were all housed in one apartment building—they were from three different East African countries, Kenya, Uganda, and Tanganyika (now Tanzania). The students were of several ethnic groups with no more in common than English, Spanish and Russian students would have, except skin color. This segregation was in keeping with an informal housing policy that placed students in dormitories and apartments based on race and religion. I ran into resistance from the director of housing. My meeting with the director ended with me walking angrily out of his office. He confided later that my exit was not a minute before he was going to throw me out. When he found out that I had the backing of West Virginia University President Paul Miller, he came rushing across campus to my office, in his shirt sleeves, to apologize. He changed the room assignment policy.

Years later when I lived in Lincoln County, West Virginia, I met the housing director's daughter was was with the back to the land movement. Much to my surprise she told me that I had caused a major change in her father's attitude toward race and segregation. I think that is karma.

We succeeded in getting the barbers union to adopt a policy of accepting customers of all races. The barbers' vote to integrate was not long after a group of us picketed a barbershop just across the street from the University. One picketer easily passed for white. He carried a sign that said, "You cut my hair, why not my brothers."

A Morgantown Chamber of Commerce brochure included in their praise of Morgantown that it was 97% white. When I pointed out the racism in that, the director didn't see my point.

As Foreign Student Advisor, I was on the Student Affairs Staff. It was announced at a staff meeting that the speaking engagement of Timothy Leary, LSD guru, was cancelled. Miss Boyd explained that it was because the university got its funding from the state legislature and they would likely cut that funding if the controversial Leary was not cancelled. I naively thought that Universities were places where controversial issues could be debated. It was a lesson in who pulls the strings.

I have since learned that the boards that control West Virginia colleges and universities include owners and executives of large corporations. The presidents and officers of West Virginia higher education institutions are often on the boards of directors of large corporations. The most recent example, reported in the March 16,

2018, edition of the *Charleston Gazette-Mail*, was the appointment of, Joyce McConnell, West Virginia University provost and vice-president of academic affairs, to the board of directors of Antero Resources, a natural gas company. Amazingly, McConnell also "serves as the chair of the West Virginia Nature Conservancy."[16] It is an eye-opener that the West Virginia Nature Conservancy website lists Antero Resources Corporation, Dominion Energy Services, Inc. and Southwestern Energy, as the three members of the Founders' Circle, reserved for donors of $25,000.[17] Makes me wonder what side the Nature Conservancy is on.

As foreign student advisor I became involved in the Regional Council on International Education. At one of our University of Pittsburgh meetings, we were addressed by a Jesuit priest. I asked the speaker about the Jesuit selling of four million slaves from Angola to Brazil. His reply was that it was only 2% of the slave trade to Brazil during the time frame that it occurred. He reduced 4,000,000 people to the number 2!

---

[16] *Charleston Gazette-Mail, March 16, 2018*
[17] *Charleston Gazette-Mail, March 16, 2018*

John Maxwell

When I was just getting started at West Virginia University as Foreign Student Advisor, I learned that John Maxwell was teaching history. We had met as freshmen at West Virginia University in 1954. I went to see him. We talked all night and finished off a fifth of bourbon.

While I was telling John about Africa, he said, "About the time you were in Africa, I had a buddy who went to Africa. When he got discharged from our Army intelligence unit in Germany, I took him down to Gibraltar and saw him off on a hitchhiking trip. His goal was to hitchhike around the perimeter of Africa."

When I was in the Peace Corps in Nigeria, my wife and I went to the Cameroon.[18] While there, we met an American hitchhiker. He had been discharged from a U.S. Army intelligence unit in Germany and a friend drove him to Gibraltar where he began hitchhiking around the perimeter of Africa.

---

[18] *The only country named for shrimp.*

Selma and James Reeb

I was asked to take a group of students to register voters in the South. I turned it down, saying that there was too much work to be done in Morgantown to try to reform some other place. That offer sounded daunting to me. I turned it down, out of fear of the racist violence used against voter registration of African-Americans. I wish I had been brave enough to have accepted that assignment.

I was barely back in West Virginia from the Peace Corps, when, on June 21, 1964, three young civil rights workers, James Chaney, Andrew Goodman, and Michael Schwerner, were murdered and buried in a Mississippi dam.

A year later, the Alabama state police gassed and beat people who were attempting a march from Selma to Montgomery for their civil rights. John Lewis, now a congressman, was beaten in the head by the police. John later married Lillian Miles, a friend from my Peace Corps group.

I was disappointed in myself that after seeing the televised beatings that I had hesitated and not gone to Selma.

The Selma march was triggered by the Alabama state police murder of Jimmy Lee Jackson. Twenty-six-year-old Jackson had recently died in a Selma hospital of wound infection, after being shot in the abdomen by a state cop. Jackson was trying to protect his mother from being beaten at Mack's Café in Marion, Alabama. Along with several other African Americans, he had taken refuge there from cops breaking up a night march protesting the arrest of James Orange, a field secretary for the *Southern Christian Leadership Conference* (SCLC).[19]

Martin Luther King, Jr., led a subsequent march that crossed the bridge out of Selma. He invited ministers and others sympathetic to the civil rights movement to join him. 500 Unitarian-Universalist ministers answered the call. One was murdered.

My Peace Corps friend, Al Ulmer, drove one of those ministers, James Reeb, from Atlanta to Selma. That evening, Reeb, Clark Olsen and Orloff Miller, all Unitarian-Universalist ministers, were

---

[19]*http://kingencyclopedia.stanford.edu/encyclopedia/encyclopedia/enc_jackson_jimmie_lee_19381965/*

attacked by white bigots on a Selma sidewalk. Reeb was killed with a baseball bat to his head.

James Reeb lived for a short time and in that time the attackers continued their terror. Clark Olsen wrote about that twenty years later:[20]

Selma was fear, reexperienced fairly often in telling friends or family about the events of that terrible night in Selma: the men coming across the street shouting angry words, carrying a club. Waiting at the clinic while the doctor examined Jim. Fearing Jim's death as he squeezed my hand more tightly as his head pain increased and before he sank into unconsciousness. Fearing for all of us when our ambulance had a flat tire just after leaving Selma's city limits on the way to the hospital in Birmingham, and the ambulance radiotelephone wouldn't work. Especially fearing when a car full of white men pulled up behind us on the country road, then followed us back to town while we drove on the rim of our flat tire, headed for a phone that would bring a replacement ambulance. Fear turned to terror when the car full of men parked next to our waiting ambulance and walked around the ambulance knocking on the windows. I thought that they might bury us in a watery ditch that night, the same kind of ditch

[20] https://www.uua.org/offices/people/clark-olsen

*where the bodies of civil rights workers James
Chaney, Andrew Goodman, and Michael
Schwerner had recently been found in Mississippi.
And fear that Jim would die before we arrived at
the Birmingham hospital.*

*....to various events and movements during
his presidency, including to Selma...[President]
Johnson's phone calls preserved at the Johnson
Library in Austin, Texas...uncovered two telling
statistics: In response to Jimmy Lee Jackson's
death, Johnson had received no phone calls; in
response to Jim Reeb's death, the President had
gotten 57 calls. [Jimmy Lee Jackson was shot by an
Alabama State policeman during a civil rights
demonstration and died in a Selma hospital. His
murder and his death on February 26, 1965
inspired the Selma march nine days later and the
Voting Rights Act of August 1965. A crowd of
25,000 people showed up for the march [led by
Martin Luther King, Jr.]*

*The murder of a young black man had
provoked little attention. The murder of a white
clergyman had moved the President and Congress
to action. Surely that was a stark lesson about the
problem of race in America. In the campaign for a
voting rights law to remedy gross racial injustices,
apparently something had to be the final straw
politically, and Jim Reeb was that symbol. Passage
of The Voting Rights Act is probably the most*

powerful legislation that, long-term, will move this country to justice for all. So many of us can be proud to have been in Selma. So many of us grieve with Jim's family that change required a last straw.

The three men who murdered Reeb were ruled innocent by an all-white, all-male Alabama jury. On March 11, 2011, 46 years after Reeb's death, *The Anniston Star* reported that the FBI was investigating the case. The killer plea bargained to a charge of manslaughter and served 6 months in prison.

I was proud of West Virginia's Ken Hechler, the only Congressman to join the Selma march. West Virginia Senator Robert Byrd, consistent with his past as a KKK organizer, didn't go to Selma.

Not long before I left for San Francisco, I heard on the radio that Martin Luther King, Jr. was murdered. Bobby Kennedy, as Attorney-General, had signed off on J. Edgar Hoover's wiretapping of King. But Kennedy seemed to have recovered his bearing and found an idealism, that would match Eugene McCarthy's less recently acquired vision. That idealism and vision probably would have elected Kennedy.

My son, after watching a documentary about Robert Kennedy said that there were no candidates talking like Kennedy—embracing the liberal philosophy. In the 2016 Democratic primary, candidate and Socialist Bernie Sanders advocated liberal populist philosophy.

Ken Hechler campaigning in his red Jeep

Playboy

I participated in a picket-line protest over *Playboy* magazine. It wasn't the West Virginia University student government raising money to send *Playboy* to soldiers in Vietnam that caused the protest. It was because the West Virginia University public relations people issued a press release bragging that West Virginia University students were pro-war. I was the only administrator in the fifteen-person student picket line. My stock went down with the university administration.

Politics

I ran for the Democratic Party nomination for County Commissioner of Monongalia County, where West Virginia University is located. In a bank I spoke to an elderly African-American lady. I told her I was for civil rights, she responded that civil rights weren't as important to her as the fact that she did not see any African-Americans working in that bank. I remembered that. I can see her now standing in front of me pointing at the all-white bank tellers—she opened my eyes.

During my campaign, the Mayor of Star City, a town near Morgantown, walked me past illegal gambling in the back room of his beer joint. Witnessing the illegal gambling, and not reporting it, compromised me from speaking out against it. And he made sure I understood that besides protection for his gambling, patronage was the price for his support. He called me and said, "If I send somebody over there for a job, you'll give it to them, right?" I answered, "If they are qualified for the job." I don't think that was the answer he wanted.

Several years later, I was working for the

Charleston YMCA. There was a summer jobs program that was supposed to be for teenagers from low-income families. The *Charleston Gazette* reported that the jobs were being given to teenagers from political connected and well-to-do families. When asked why that was so, the County Commissioners claimed that they didn't get any applications from poor kids.

I and Ed Edmunds, who worked with low-income teenagers at the North Charleston recreation center, handed out applications to low-income kids and got five hundred filled out.

Jack Catalano, president of the county commission, called and said he wanted me and the YMCA to run the summer jobs program. I said we would. He then said, "If I send someone over there for one of the jobs, you will give it to them, right?"

There it was; I could say, yes, certainly mister commissioner, and be part of the good old boys' network of cooperating sycophants. It was intimidating, but I am glad I said, "If they are next in line." It wasn't the answer he wanted.

The influence of politicians in the selection process was the very reason the summer jobs program needed to be changed. I did not hear from him again about the YMCA and me running the summer jobs program. But they did hire a lot of the participants from our five hundred applications.

If it is possible to come in a close third, I did that in the race for the Monongalia county commission. The incumbent won by about two hundred votes, a young coal miner came in second and I was close behind him. By running for that office, I probably took some votes away from the coal miner, allowing the incumbent to win—not my intention.

After the election, I ran into my coal miner opponent in downtown Morgantown. He said he spent $200 for whiskey in the election and asked how much I had spent. I guess he was surprised that I spent nothing on whiskey. I was surprised he was so honest about election fraud. Is honesty about dishonesty a virtue?

I was probably lucky to have lost that election because what I had in mind would have brought the roof down on me. Had I been nominated and elected, I was going to try to get property taxes raised on coal, limestone companies and other industries, and eliminated for home owners. I figured, and still do, that a person should only have to pay for their home one time and never be in danger of losing it because they couldn't pay their property taxes.

Property tax on your home means you are renting it from the local government. Miss your tax payments and the county can take your property and put it up for auction on the court house steps, where alert politicians and coal companies, who are often the same people, buy it at bargain prices.

"It"

I think it was 1964 that I was driving from Morgantown to Charleston, when I saw it for the first time. "It," was a strip mine. I pulled over, stopped the car, got out and tried not to believe my eyes. There was a great gash around the side of the mountain. It looked like the mountain had been horse-collared. I could not believe anyone would get on a bulldozer and do that.

I gasp every time I see mountain top removal strip mining. People whom I take to see it most often in a hushed voice say, "Oh my god," when they first see the destruction. They may wonder if there *is* a god when they look out and down into a root canal being done on a mountain with a nine-story dragline and two-story dump trucks—trucks so large they have stairs to get to the driver's cabin and the dragline has a sleeping place and kitchen. However, one visitor did say that "it" wasn't so bad because it was where no one could see it.

From my days as Foreign Student Adviser at West Virginia University I knew the man who would later be appointed director of the West Virginia Department of Natural Resources which regulated strip mining. I called him to complain about strip mining and he said I was obsessed with strip mining. That was the kind of diagnoses Soviet Union officials came to about dissidents—they were declared crazy. I got off easy, the Soviets put their crazy dissidents in insane asylums.

Dragline Amidst its Destruction of Kayford Mountain[21] *Photo by Vivian Stockman*

---

[21]*https://ohvec.org/links/news/archive/2005/fair_use/03_09.html*

Dragline bucket with 60-member marching band

Open for Business

It is so crazy, blowing up the mountains in the mountain state. Governor Joe Manchin changed the state motto appearing on billboards welcoming visitors from *Wild and Wonderful* to *Open for Business*, as if that wasn't obvious from the massive destruction wrought by coal, timber, natural gas, and chemical businesses. Looks like someone left the door open a long time ago and Manchin was rubbing our nose in it.

For Manchin to think that Open for Business was a good idea told me something about his intelligence. As a former coal broker, Manchin's allegiance was obvious for a long time. Public outrage forced him to return to *Wild and Wonderful,* which itself had been invented by public relations hacks, under Governor Arch Moore to replace *The Mountain State* motto.

Arch Moore eventually spent three years in federal prison for lying and stealing. Long before Moore went to prison, Governor Wally Barron set a high bar. He got caught bribing the head juror in a trail in which Barron was being tried for bribery.

In Love

In 1965 I fell in love with Stanli Mitchell, an African-American student. I was twenty-six and she was twenty-two. Although there were no written rules against West Virginia University faculty or administrators falling in love with students, I feared that I had stepped across a line.

We flew below the radar until the morning of her graduation day. We held hands and walked down High Street and into Comuntzis' restaurant for breakfast. There sat her boss, the chairman of the civil engineering department. Stanli was a part time secretary in his office. (I saw her type a term paper in one setting, no revision.)

We joined her boss for breakfast. We were out of the closet. Before that the closest we came to revealing our relationship to other than some good friends was when Stanli delivered my birthday presents to my parents in St. Albans.

After graduation, Stanli worked for the Job Corps in Charleston. We went out to dinner at *Clements* beside the Kanawha River, just a short distance up river from Charleston. After dinner, we walked, holding hands, in nearby Daniel Boone

Park. We passed three elderly white men one of whom looked down as we passed. Years later my sister told me that the man who looked down was our grandpa Charlie Barker.

Poverty Banquet

I attended an oxy-moronic poverty "banquet." There were some people there from Beria College in Kentucky. Berea was Johnny Skees' home town. Johnny is an amazing character. I wrote about him in *Imagonna: Peace Corps Memories.* After his Peace Corps service, Johnny smuggled Spanish brandy from the island of Sao Tome, while doing volunteer work at Albert Schweitzer's hospital.

I asked the Berea people if they knew Johnny. Indeed, they did. They told me that Johnny worked for an anti-poverty organization in Berea. At a bargain price he bought a fine-looking old Buick.

He got lost on a dirt road in the hills of Eastern Kentucky and pulled up beside a man who was walking along the edge of the road. With the push of a button, Johnny lowered the passenger side window. The man gave him directions to his intended destination and then asked, "What line of work are you in."

Johnny proudly answered, "I'm in the war on poverty."

The man studied the lush leather interior of the Buick and replied, "It looks like you are winning."

I asked the time. The Beria people gave me a one-hour earlier time from watches tuned to the central time zone. After the "banquet," I was one hour late for a date with Stanli Mitchell, she wasn't happy.

Kiyoshi Ohama

Kiyoshi Ohama, a student at West Virginia University, was from the Reyukyu Islands. I had to look it up. Okinawa, Kiyoshi's home, was one of those islands south of Japan. Kiyoshi didn't speak English well. He had read and loved John Steinbeck. With little English to exchange, I would say, "Tortilla Flat" and we both smiled and shook our heads up and down. Then he would say, "Cannery Row," to the same affect.

Before his first year was up, Kiyoshi feared he had been used by the Institute for International Education, the organization that paid all his expenses, and the American military, that had flown him to the United States. He decided to go home to join in activities against the United States military presence on Okinawa.

When Kiyoshi arrived in San Francisco he sent me this letter:

Jan. 20, 1965, Hotel Stratford, San Francisco
Dear Mr. Martin
How are you, sir?
I am quite fine and enjoy my final trip in U.S.A. I arrived here San Francisco on 18th at around 2:am

I had the telephone number of IIE [Institute for International Education], however, my arrival was so early that I made my mind to spend a couple of hours at airport.

It was not only I that spent there for killing hours of nuisance at free fee: a pretty amount of soldiers who boarded the same air line of mine were sleeping on the chairs. I chuckled for the first time since I left Morgantown, for I succeeded my plan. Because again I had to take advantage of my dressing-up stile that did not display me non-money-student type of tourist (I had only $39). Mrs. Doane[22] must giggle to know this. There was another fear beside the famous four Fears: as for me, everyday conversation of English had been a tremendously damned fear. I had to save money there (AirPort). Hotels were available if I called. But I kept on silence before the serial telephone sets which called directly to each hotel, I was afraid that my poor business English would make me run out of my total at once.

I had much tie [time] before the dawn. I sauntered at every nook and corner in the air terminal thousand times. Sometimes I bought a chewing gum. I took coffee twice; I said good morning twice. The waitress seeming Japanese smiled twice and served me a lot of coffee. I was so happy. I

---

[22] *Mrs. Doane preceded me as a part-time foreign student advisor.*

showed at such and such and then I slept comfortably on the chairs.

West Virginia was covered with white YUKI on my leaving day. But San Francisco none but people. I went to San Francisco IIE[23] at 8:00 a.m. I used Lift for the first time. I took a an [man] and asked him how to operate that machine. He as kind enough not to laugh at that country fellow. I remembered that one that one thing that I disliked to go to the library was that I didn't not know how to operate its lift when I was the student of W.V.U.

Dear Mr. Martin, I am to leave here on the 22nd, January by MATS.[24] I am very happy to spend three more days in this city. How is you cold? IIE disbursed non-school maintainance up to the departure of mine.

Thank you.

Sincerely yours

Kiyoshi Ohama

---

[23] *Institute for International Education*
[24] *Military Air Transport Service*

The Day They Closed International House

I helped organize the Student Action for Appalachian Progress (SAAP), a tutoring and community action group. Originally, I had named it Student Action Against Appalachian Poverty, but the students asked that the name be changed because they felt uncomfortable saying the name to the poor people they were working with.

Some of the students in SAAP organized a chapter of Students for a Democratic Society (SDS). The national SDS organization required five students as charter members to start a chapter. Only four were willing to risk that. I agreed to be the fifth charter member.

An acting West Virginia University president followed the very capable Paul Miller. The acting President and his Morgantown Chamber of Commerce kin, took Senator Robert Byrd around to view the things he had made possible with his skill at the pork barrel. At every stop, the SDS greeted the group with signs objecting to honoring a Klan organizer.

When the acting President saw me, he looked like he might get sick. I was obviously out of control. He would cure that.

Former University President Paul Miller, who by then was an assistant Secretary of Education in Washington, D.C., was sent to represent the federal government at the graduation ceremony where Senator Robert Byrd was to be given an honorary doctorate.

Miller had signed off on hiring me at West Virginia University and encouraged me to be bold. Once, in a chance meeting in downtown Morgantown, he shook my hand and said, "I like young Turks."

Miller's new wife, and her children, walked with him toward the graduation ceremony. He saw me in the SDS picket line against Byrd and stopped. He shook my hand and introduced his new family. The Associated Press photographer took a picture of Miller shaking my hand —I held a picket sign in my other hand. Several years later, Kitty Melville, who had been a reporter for the Daily Athenaeum student newspaper, told me that the AP people were warned that if they used that picture, they would never get another story from the University.

While we picketed outside the graduation ceremony, the graduating social work students stood and turned their backs on Byrd as he was being honored by the acting President.

One week later, I was invited to a meeting with the university financial people. They wanted to know, since it wasn't supporting itself, why they shouldn't close International House. I pointed out that hardly anything at West Virginia University was self-supporting.

Going by their standards, only the football and basketball teams would be left. They didn't look up from their figures. They had orders and just needed to go through the motions.

David Hess, director of Student Educational Services, and my boss, refused the acting President's request that he fire me. The acting president closed International House and I was banished, with no annual pay raise and a feeling I would never get one, to a windowless balcony in the old Mountainlair. That decaying building was a large Navy-surplus dining hall in the hollow behind the wonderful old Mountaineer Field.

Proud to Have Been in the Klan

While running for the West Virginia House of Representatives in 1952, Robert Byrd said that he was no longer a member of the Klan. As a West Virginia University student in 1956, I heard Congressman Byrd give a speech at Morgantown's First Baptist Church. Byrd pounded a Bible with his fist to illustrate that like an anvil, it had withstood the hammers of fascism, communism and such.

After the speech a man in the back of the chapel made a statement about the KKK. Byrd replied and admitted he had been a member of the Klan. He said that the *Charleston Gazette* had exposed this to try to ruin him. He went on to say that he was, "proud to have been a member of the Klan," I heard him say that. Byrd had joined the Ku Klux Klan in 1942 and held the offices of Exalted Cyclops[25] and Kleagle.[26] Strange aside: Byrd was one of two West Virginia legislators to witness the first execution in the electric chair at Moundsville prison.

---

[25] *Each local chapter, or Klavern, is led by an Exalted Cyclops.*
[26] *Recruiter*

Below in italics, was written three months before I resigned as West Virginia University Foreign Student Advisor and headed for San Francisco. My exodus was encouraged by the new West Virginia University administration after I participated in that picket protest at the 1967 graduation ceremonies objecting to the awarding of an honorary doctorate to Senator Robert Byrd.

In 1944, Byrd wrote to segregationist Mississippi Senator Theodore Bilbo: "I shall never fight in the armed forces with a Negro by my side... Rather I should die a thousand times, and see Old Glory trampled in the dirt never to rise again, than to see this beloved land of ours become degraded by race mongrels, a throwback to the blackest specimen from the wilds."

Byrd later wrote a letter to the Grand Wizard of the KKK saying, "The Klan is needed today as never before and I am anxious to see its rebirth here in West Virginia and in every state in the nation."

While running for the House of Representatives in 1952 Byrd said that he was no longer a member of the clan and was not interested in it. In 1956, I heard Byrd say, after a patriotic speech to a Baptist Church in Morgantown, that he was proud to have been a member of the Klan.

While on the house committee that oversaw the District of Columbia, Byrd made gratuitous and racist entries into the Congressional Record that were damaging to the African-American population of the District.

When it was no longer expedient for Byrd to be a racist he shifted gears and hired an African-American staff member.

Byrd's most memorable political actions were to filibuster the *Civil Rights Act* of 1964 and vote against the *Voting Rights Act* of 1965. *Citizens Against Government Waste* crowned Byrd the, "King of Pork," dismissing the billions of federal dollars he sent to West Virginia as worthless "Byrd droppings."[27] Near the end of his life, Byrd was the only U.S. Senator to oppose the war on Iraq and he finally spoke up against the coal companies for whom he had carried water throughout his political career.[28]

Apologists for Byrd have portrayed him as having reformed since the days when he was the organizer for the Klan in southern West Virginia

---

[27] *https://www.csmonitor.com/From-the-news-wires/2010/0628/Sen.-Robert-Byrd-King-of-pork-or-larger-than-life-hero*

[28] *blogs.wvgazettemail.com/coaltattoo/2009/12/03/sen-byrd-coal-must-embrace-the-future/*

and when he would gratuitously enter into the Congressional Record the negative data that he could scrape off the bottom of his intellectual barrel about African-Americans living in the District of Columbia.

Before I took the hint, resigned, and lit out for San Francisco, I got in one last punch at West Virginia University racism. The day after Martin Luther King, Jr. was murdered, a group of African American students gathered in Woodburn Circle held hands and expressed their feelings to comfort one another.

The West Virginia University student government president led a group of White student leaders and addressed the mourning students. He said something like, "I am willing to help in any way I can." He didn't respond when I asked, "Can they join your fraternity?"

Author's update—I more recently heard Byrd speaking on so-called[29] public radio. It was the twentieth century Byrd, not quite to his welcome twenty-first century stand against the Iraq War.

---

[29] *"So-called," because Public Radio is now financed mainly by big business.*

And neither was it the Byrd that the *Charleston Gazette* made fun of for wearing baggy suits in his early days at the state legislature. He was telling Congress of the need for straight roads in West Virginia.

He lamented the crooked roads that follow creek and river bottoms. He didn't see the value in them being picturesque or in going past locally owned businesses. He wanted our poor citizens to be able to travel on them big ol' four lanes that go straight through everything.

Of course, he didn't mention that the coal and timber trucks would have an easier time of carrying the state away to our lords in other states. Neither did he mention that the sons and daughters of those lords in other states could more readily get to our remaining natural wonders.

In his story The Bear, William Faulkner observed that the two-lane hardtops being built into the Mississippi wilderness would destroy what was worth seeing or feeling in the first place. It's like the Heisenberg uncertainty principle—looking at something changes it. During a speech opening a portion of a boondoggle highway called Corridor H, Byrd swept his arm toward the mountains behind him and spoke of them in his grandiose style not noticing he was drawing attention to a mountain that had been strip-mined.

Byrd was concerned about the average citizen and his struggle in getting to the mall. But, more than that, he was probably looking over his shoulder at campaign support from the highway construction companies and votes he would get for creating construction jobs. Senator Byrd and the Snopes family: moving right along into the twenty-first century.

Byrd has recently redeemed himself. He has apologized for his racism and for voting for the Gulf of Tonkin resolution. He was the only Senator to oppose the war on Iraq.

In May of 2010 Byrd wrote that, "The industry of coal must also respect the land that yields the coal, as well as the people who live on the land. If the process of mining destroys nearby wells and foundations, if blasting and digging and relocating streams unearths harmful elements and releases them into the environment causing illness and death, that process should be halted and the resulting hazards to the community abated."[30]

---

[30] *blogs.wvgazettemail.com/coaltattoo/2009/12/03/sen-byrd-coal-*

I was 26 years old and back from two years in the Peace Corps and had just started as the first full-time foreign student advisor at West Virginia University. Some of the following letters to the editor chapters show what must have been a lack of concern about losing my job.

The Sheriff's Bumper Stickers

The Morgantown Post
May 6, 1964

Dear Sirs,

As a private, tax-paying citizen, I would like to comment on a campaign tactic I have observed in Monongalia County. I notice that the Sheriff's cars have stickers advertising the campaign of one of our gubernatorial candidates. The Sheriff told me when I called him that he saw nothing unethical about this. He said he owned those cars himself and even bought the sheriff's emblems that are on the doors.

I asked him if it is unethical to use a sheriff's car for campaigning during the day when the people driving them were on official duty and when the taxpayers of this county were paying their salaries and seven cents a mile. He replied that one cannot operate a car on seven cents a mile and that he did not consider it unethical to juxtaposition the official sheriff's emblem and the campaign sign. He said, patronizingly, that the car was his and that he had the right to campaign for whomever he pleased.

It seems to me that during the normal duty hours of an elected public official it is quite unethical to use a vehicle for both official county matters and political campaigning, regardless of who owns the vehicle.

Cecil Rhodes and Economic Advancement in Rhodesia

Morgantown Post
November 16, 1965

Dear Editor

In your editorial of November 15 entitled "The Rhodesian Situation," you indicate that a new deterrent will be created to keep advanced nations from going "…into the backward areas of the world to…take the lead in working for their economic and social advancement." The advanced nation of Great Britain never went into Rhodesia in the first place.

A charter company headed by Cecil Rhodes first went into Rhodesia without any intention of working for their economic and social advancement. Rhodes' company was there for one reason—to get rich. The best land was forcibly taken from the Matabele and Mashona tribes. Rhodes' company first expected to find gold and when this dream did not pan out they turned to land speculation.

They encouraged immigration to sell the fertile land they expropriated from the Africans. The only economic advancement that has been worked for since that time has been the advancement of the white settlers at the expense and on the labor of the Africans.

The settlers worked so hard for their own economic advancement that by 1957 the average per capita annual income for a white person in Rhodesia was about $2,000 compared to $40 for the average African. And the whites, comprising 9% of the population, controlled 50% of the land (which happened to be the most fertile 50%) while the Africans, comprising 90% of the population, were confined to 22%.

The whites were only cultivating 2.5% of the land they held—the rest was involved in land speculation by absentee landlords. Enough for the economic advancement of Rhodesia.

As for social advancement, the Europeans had done such a good job by 1958 that of three million Africans in Southern Rhodesia only about 1,695 could vote. The European Rhodesians were receiving fifteen times as much per capita for education than were the Africans.

Your editorial sounded as if you thought the Africans of Rhodesia ought to be more grateful for the way the white settlers have taken their land, exploited their labor at below subsistence wages, and robbed them of their dignity.

The part of Rhodesia now called Zimbabwe has descended into a hell that the former White settlers might point to with an "I told you so." Mugabe's government has taken revenge on the White settlers. He has turned the place into a police state dealing harshly with any opposition. By 2008 starvation and cholera were added to the woes of the people of Zimbabwe. In 2018 president Mugabe resigned and his vice-president, a Mugabe enforcer has been elected president.

Aesthetic Idiots

The Daily Athenaeum
November 10, 1966

Dear Editor,

   With little doubt in mind I believe that we have a bunch of aesthetic idiots destroying what physical beauty this university has. I bit my tongue when the horribly ugly physical plant building was set up on the Evansdale Campus, and when the bare asphalt parking lot at the Medical Center Apartments was enlarged. But today comes the revolution. A giant ugly asphalt parking lot has been placed on the field in front of the Medical Center totally ruining the aesthetic quality of that building.

   Parking lots can be built with proper landscaping that will be beautiful to look at, such as the original lot around the Medical Center. However the new one has no landscaping within the lot and don't be surprised if there is none put around it.

   Almost everyone to whom I talk about the subject of campus beauty is disgusted with what is happening. Students are disgusted because there is no place for recreation. There is plenty of asphalt for parking lots but none for outdoor basketball and tennis courts.

We have 900 students in the Twin Towers and not one recreational facility—but baby we've got parking lots all over hell out there. We need large playing fields, parks, benches, sidewalks—but all we get are ugly parking lots that are fast chewing up the landscape.

Townspeople are disgusted with how the beauty of their town is being ruined and they are wondering what horrors the University has in mind for the Morgantown Golf and Country Club property. If the University can do no better than this, it ought to get out while there is still some semblance of beauty in Evansdale.

The Evansdale Campus had a chance of being beautiful when the Medical Center was built and then it was ruined with the totally graceless engineering building. Now we have the "tin can" there and asphalt strips everywhere—next we will probably let someone build a junkyard.

I'm sure that if there was a river running through the Evansdale campus that we would pollute it and brag that we have the only polluted river on any campus in the United States. I fully expect to see a strip-mine operation most any day begin on what is left of all that grass and stuff on our campus.

Now [2018], the area around the WVU medical school is infested with gaudy fast food joints, franchise businesses and a hodgepodge of cheaply built condos and apartments. The country club property mentioned in my letter now has a football stadium named for a man who gave the most money.

Pesticides and Patriotism

To the Appalachian Center at West Virginia University
January 17, 1968.

> *(This was written three months before I resigned as West Virginia University Foreign Student Advisor and headed for San Francisco. My exodus was encouraged by the new WVU administration after I participated in the protest at the 1967 graduation ceremony.)*

This letter is in response to your cover letter of January 1966 to Mr. Lewis McLean's speech on pesticides and fertilizers. I thought Mr. McLean had some sound arguments for the use of pesticides but am at a loss to understand why he chose to not so subtly associate those who are against the use of pesticides with hippies and insinuate that critics are un-American. This line of argument was not necessary to get his point across.

I cannot understand why people choose to destroy the character of those who disagree with their point of view. It might be more intellectual and worthier of a publication produced by the Appalachian Center to print speeches and reports that stick with the substance of issues and refrain from character assassination.

It appears that, perhaps, Mr. McLean did have an ax to grind, for on the first page of the speech he seems to be addressing himself to fertilizer dealers, which leads me to believe that he was seeking their approval.

I find it distasteful that you believe that it is important to recognize the "character" of those who are against pesticides or man-made synthetics. Character has nothing to do with an opinion on such subjects and whether a man is for or against pesticides has nothing to do with whether he is American or un-American, hippy or non-hippy.

I never in my wildest nightmares expected to see the American flag waved in a speech on pesticides and chemicals—unless of course, the speaker has a vested interest in promoting the sale of pesticides and chemicals.[31]

---

[31] *I later learned that Mr. McLean was speaking under the sponsorship of Velsicol Chemical Corporation.*

Monongalia County, 1965
Unpublished

Today I saw the Humphrey mine belching large quantities of foul colored smoke into the air. It appears from their activities that coal companies in this area own the streams and the air. They are intent on destroying both the air and water and endangering those of us who drink and bathe in their acid mine water and breathe their smoke-filled air.

Perhaps the air was stolen at the same time they stole the once beautiful Monongahela, killed its fish and began to feed us the acid mine water. They even told us that we were lucky because the mine acid was killing the bacteria in the water. It was as if they dumped the acid into the river to counter the shit, in a spasm of civic responsibility.

The coal interests take our coal almost free of taxes. They pollute our air and streams and seduce our politicians.

Coal barons don't build anything more lasting and beautiful than a rusted-out coal tipple or a mountain top stripped bare of its natural beauty. They ask us to consider them our number one asset.

Light Shed on Controversy
The Daily Athenaeum
November 4, 1966

The following two articles appeared side by side on the front page of the Daily Athenaeum, the student newspaper at West Virginia University. I was informed that the coach was going to write a column concerning the allegation that the African American basketball players were told not to date White girls. I did not see the coach's article in advance of publication and was not told of its contents.

This editor's note preceded the two articles: In a sermon decrying campus apathy last Sunday, the Rev. Michael Paine mentioned Negro basketball players were warned against dating White girls. Here, the two sides of the issue are presented by Julian Martin as the source of Paine's comments and by the head basketball coach.

My article:

On October 21, 1966, I sent a memo to some of my colleagues, including some of the campus ministers, in which I asked them if they would believe that the Negro basketball players had been told not to date white girls because it would be bad for the image.

Michael Paine included this information in his sermon after I confirmed to him that the information was true. I was informed that a group meeting had been called of Negro basketball players and that during that time it was made clear that the Negro basketball players should not date white girls.

It seems that this "understanding" was carried to the extent of calling in a Negro basketball player and asking him about the "white" girl he was seen with—ironically, the girl was white in color but Negro by our interesting method of classifying people.

This must make it difficult on the Negro student trying to figure out who is white and who isn't, especially when about 85 % of southern "white" people have some Negro ancestry. [*85% is much too high--I took a friend's word.[32]*]

As this argument progresses don't be surprised to hear such qualified statements as "the head coach didn't make such a statement," or "no one ever said that to us." But bear in mind that no one has accused anyone of making any particular statement. There are many ways to make a point clear without being direct—this is not to say that the Negro basketball players were not told directly, just that no one has made that accusation.

---

[32] *See black/?utm_term=.39c8e13c41ae*
https:www.washingtonpost.com/news/wonk/wp/2014/12/22/a-lot-of-southern-whites-are-a-little-bit

The sad part of the whole controversy is that in our concern with "image," our culture is mainly concerned with how one dresses and how one behaves publicly rather than whether or not one is really spiritually and intellectually growing.

Why not encourage the Negro athletes to foster the "image" of the brotherhood of man across the state by being seen dating whomever they want to date without reference to race, color or creed?

Perhaps by copying the total "image" of the basketball team the youngsters of our state would not only learn to dress in a neat and clean manner but might also learn to grow up without harboring the subtle hate that prevents one race from dating or marrying another.

The Coach's Article:

It is with great disappointment that I reply to public accusations of the administration of our basketball program.

To publicly portray a lack of mutual respect between player and coach and imply an unwholesome rapport between any individuals in our program without the courage or slightest effort to substantiate the facts with me is of great concern.

The word "alleged" cannot vindicate the total irresponsibility of this act.

We do not always expect to be correct, but as long as we reside in the United States, we hope that our position will be accurately determined before being held up to public scorn. It is distressing to have to defend young men who need no defense and an issue that never existed, but it is apparent that I must clarify an injustice.

My position in regard to the social life of our athletes has been clearly defined—for them and for anyone else who wishes to know. Their areas of responsibility are as follows:
1) Strict adherence to the training regulations.
2) Their appearance will be exemplary because they have pride in themselves and our program.
3) Their conduct will always be that of a gentleman representing a god-fearing and wholesome organization and the youth of our state would do well to emulate them.

These are the only areas of their lives we try to influence.

We have complete confidence in their ability to manage their own personal lives as they have proven this without question to anyone who has had the pleasure of contact with our young men.

No university possesses a coaching staff or squad that strives harder than ours to attain success in our field of competition and we do not apologize for that. However, as long as I am directing the program, we will never lose sight of the important role we have in projecting the image of our University and state.

Millions of people will see, hear or read about our program. These same people may never see our campus, meet our president or speak with our students and faculty. They will probably not know how many volumes are in our library and, in fact, may never set foot in our state. To these people we are more than just individuals who play basketball—we represent a university and a state.

I confess that our program is guilty of being concerned with image and it has and will continue to bring pride to our school and our state both on and off the court.

To preserve the dignity of our program, there will be no more statements or contributions to perpetuate this "alleged" controversy

Excerpts from the Philosophy Department Chair's Response:

...Does the following limpid paragraph from your letter imply that the Negro basketball players were not warned against dating white girls?

"We have complete confidence in their ability to manage their own personal lives as they have proven this without question to anyone who has had the pleasure of contact with our young men."

....you outline in your letter three "areas of responsibility" which clearly defines your position "in regard to the social life of our athletes."

The traditional objective of a university as you know, is the disinterested pursuit of knowledge and truth

The second area refers to the appearance of our athletes and the third refers to their conduct....THE ONLY "IMAGE" that a university should worry about is whether this traditional objective is preserved and fostered

....If "image of a university" implies exemplary appearance, then I suppose Albert Einstein would have been a bad representative of our university—he wore neither tie or socks.

If "image of the university" implies the kind of conduct exhibited by "a gentleman representing a God-fearing and wholesome organization." Neither atheists, Calvinists nor agnostics in the student body or on the staff would be good representatives of West Virginia University....This sort of thing is out of place at a "real" university.

Dick Hudson, the Charleston Daily Mail sports editor, wrote this:

As for some heckling in the WVU wings by the beatniks, Coach Waters' basketball PROGRAM IS SOUND and the image is good. He'll continue to insist that the players dress neatly, have haircuts and try to be decent gents no matter what some ministers, sandal-clad advisors[33] or philosophy professors may say.

---

[33] *I did have long hair and sometimes wore sandals.*

To San Francisco

In the late spring of 1968 Joan Breiding and I left Morgantown, West Virginia, on a trip that would eventually take us to San Francisco. We pitched a tent in a Kentucky state park and experienced hundreds of mosquitos in a Memphis park too close to the Mississippi River. We saw no white people in that Memphis park—that miserable site was reserved for African-Americans.

A few miles north of Vicksburg, Mississippi, something was wrong with my old huge tail-finned Chrysler Imperial. Every bump was magnified up into my back. We spotted a car parts sign and stopped.

It was a huge barn with hundreds of used car parts in piles, on the walls and hanging from the roof. After an inspection the owner told me that the car had a broken leaf spring. His men found one in the labyrinth of old car parts.

While the spring was being replaced, the White owner mentioned a newspaper report of a recent civil rights demonstration and nodded in the direction of some shouting and said, "That's what they are taught."

When I asked the owner how much I owed him for replacing the spring, he looked at my Eugene McCarthy for President bumper sticker and said it was twenty dollars. He added that if it had been a George Wallace bumper sticker it would have been ten dollars but for a Kennedy sticker it would be fifty dollars.

After I paid him he asked where we were going. California, I answered. He said, "If I came to a sign that said California in one direction and hell in the other, I would go to hell."

In New Orleans we visited a priest, whom we knew when he was at Newman House at West Virginia University in Morgantown.

In Houston we stopped and visited Norman Gary, my best friend from Peace Corps days. The Breiding family cat rode that far with us and then disappeared.

Galveston was next with puddles of oil all over the beach. Later I wrote a letter to the Galveston Chamber of Commerce and told them how much fun it was trying to walk on an oil covered beach.

Somewhere, we were parked on a main street, sleeping, Joan on top of our stuff in the back seat and me in the front seat. We woke up to a police car loud-speaker and a flashing blue light from behind us. To my relief the cops were speaking to the car parked in front of us. We went back to sleep.

We stopped at Carlsbad Caverns. I remember that on the elevator taking us down to the caverns, an old man let go with a round of putt-putt farts— now at 82, I remember him when I do the putt-putts.

Just as we crossed into Arizona, a state police car followed us. I handed a brandy bottle to a smelly hitch-hiker riding with us and told him to jam it down in our stuff that was packed in the back seat. I ate a banana to hide the brandy smell on my breath and then pulled over, as suggested by the flashing blue light, to be interviewed by a state cop. I lied when I answered his question, "How much have you had to drink."

I decided to enter California via Mono Lake. The map showed a 62-mile road from Hawthorne, Nevada, to Mono Lake in California. There were no people, no gas stations, nothing but high-altitude dry, hot, desert country. It wasn't real smart to take that old Chrysler Imperial across that no man's land. This was before cell phones and we didn't see a house or another car the whole way.

Mono Lake has strange salt formations, nothing like I had ever seen. Because there is no outlet, it is saltier than the oceans. Brine shrimp and alkali flies flourish and attract massive bird migrations and nesting. Only the Great Salt Lake hosts more nesting California gulls than Mono Lake.[34]

Mono Lake

[34] *Wikipedia*

California Sea Gulls at Mono Lake

Just after near 7,000-foot Mono Lake we
passed through Tioga Pass at almost 10,000 feet
with eight-foot high snow banks on both sides of
the road.

Finally, we saw the promised land. Across the
bay, San Francisco was pastels, fog, and spackled
sun. It felt good.

Delores Huerta

In 1969, Delores Huerta, a founder, along with Caesar Chavez, of the United Farmworkers Union, came to a picket line I was in at the San Francisco headquarters of a large grape-growing company.

She said, "Let's go upstairs and talk to them, ask them why they don't treat their workers better." It had not occurred to me that I could do that, that it was ok to go right in their offices and talk with the people working there.

One of the office staff admitted that if he considered moral implications he would quit his job. That visit emboldened me and led me for the rest of my life to be less intimidated by power.

Getting to that picket line resulted from meeting Ray Pena' on the San Francisco beach. Ray had lost his car keys somewhere in the sand. I drove him home to get spares. He was an organizer for the United Farmworkers Union and got me involved. This led to me driving Chicano[35] voters to the polls in the Mission District, on June 5, 1968, to vote for Robert Kennedy. That evening I saw the report on TV of Kennedy being murdered—I screamed and yelled in anger and frustration.

---

[35] *Chicano is the name Ray called himself and other Mexican-Americans.*

W L

Ping! Ping! Ping! Things metallic hit near me. I looked around. A couple more pings. A small nail rolled on the sidewalk. I picked it up and looked across the street. Three kids were glaring at me. I had no big city experience—I didn't know whom to fear. I walked across the street and held out the nail, expecting they would look at it.

"Did you throw this?" I asked.

"Ain't nobody throw nuthun." No eye contact. They ignored the nail in my outstretched hand. A bigger brother came out of their basement home. Through a drugged beer haze and eyes jerking back and forth, he said, "What, throw what, who, man."

"Don't let it happen again," I said, and walked away.

The following week, I saw those kids at the basketball court outside the gothic St. Michael Greek Orthodox church. I approached their game. They recognized me. I was the white boy they had thrown nails at—the one who crossed the street and told them to quit it.

I was a decent basketball player and older than the kids. The next day they brought out two older brothers to offer me some competition. I found out their last name was Sproul.

Brother Paul was lean, quick, and a better player than me. Brother W L was clumsy at basketball and had no idea what the rules were. He dribbled with both hands at the same time, ran with the ball and shot it so hard that the rebound sometimes went all the way to the centerline.

Paul was a good basketball player, but he looked like he would rather be drinking malt liquor. There was no trust in his pale-blue jerking eyes. Paul didn't say anything. He didn't smile nor respond to smiles and didn't answer when I spoke to him. He never came back to the court after that one day.

W L was a big, handsome man, with the soft muscles of a weight lifter gone to chubby. He wore a black leather jacket, black pants, a black beret and dark sunglasses—on TV he had seen Black Panthers in Oakland dressed that way. He strutted self-consciously and swayed side to side.

Taps on his heels made a special cocky sound as he strummed down the street, singing to himself.

His swagger made up for not being athletic or book smart. It was profitable for both his pocketbook and his Id. Hippies in the area were intimidated and willing to buy him off with free dope. His size, the Black Panther fantasy, and his swagger, got him by. But he had a childlike trust that lived beneath the swagger.

W L showed me a scar where he said a bullet had gone in his side. I pieced together from our conversations that his adolescent school days were spent in youth detention centers.

W L told me that his mother moved to San Francisco from Mississippi in 1950. While Momma Sproul was working two jobs, there was a swarm of kids in their basement apartment with no adult to look after them during the day. They stayed up late, smoked dope, drank beer, dropped pills, and slept past noon. They only went to school to score some dope or take some kid's lunch money. Momma was too worn out from work to do anything with them.

The Breiding family and I moved from California Street to a larger house, a faux Victorian on Bush Street, not far from the Fillmore Auditorium where the Jefferson Airplane, the Mommas and the Pappas, Country Joe and the Fish,

Buffalo Springfield, Bob Dylan, and all the great and near-great rock and rollers held forth. I was never inside the Fillmore, never heard or saw in person any of those icons of the hippie wars.

Joe, another of W L's older brothers, showed up and lent his considerable muscularity to carrying furniture the two blocks of the move. He was a pleasant fellow, smiled graciously and came back later to my basement apartment and demanded a payment of marijuana for his moving services. He made it clear that he would beat the hell out of me if I didn't give him some dope.

I appealed to Joe's understanding. "Hey, everybody upstairs will know. Some of them were in the next room when you came in. They heard you ask for dope. If I go up there and get the dope and bring it to you, they will know that I was forced to do it. They will know that you disrespected me. Tomorrow I'll meet you up the street and give you the dope, but that has to be the last time. Is that a deal?" He diverted his eyes and said, "Yeah, that's a deal." He left without taking my offer of a handshake.

San Francisco is a small city. Two blocks from the Sproul swarm of poverty was the elegant

Pacific Heights. In 1968 poor and rich lived two blocks apart. There were many opportunities for a poor kid to make a living breaking into homes, mugging hippies on the street, and selling dope.

Like big brother W L, the other Sproul brothers were experienced street hustlers. There was money to be made terrorizing neighborhood hippies, who often had some dope worth stealing. They watched hippie backyards for signs of marijuana plants they could steal.

The hippies had no protection. They couldn't complain to the police about a stolen marijuana plant. I don't think that the police cared who won in a conflict between "hippies and niggers." Police advice to us was to "shoot the niggers," if they forced their way into the house, but "make sure they are inside."

Once the cops found out that a house was a hippie pad, they didn't bother answering calls for help. I imagined them saying, let 'em fight it out. Maybe they will all kill each other. Good riddance.

The Breidings learned from more experienced hippies that the best protection was to call the fire department. Firemen were obliged to answer fire reports in San Francisco, even hippie pads, because every house in "The City" seemed to be connected—and most were made of wood torn from forests farther north. The cops were obliged to go to fires to protect the firemen.

W L and I became friends. With W L as my protector, I could go safely anywhere in the Fillmore district. Nobody messed with Mr. badass swagger W L. I think that at times W L was showing me off, as if I was his queer white friend, his punk. He pointed to what he wanted, usually malt liquor, and ordered it in a loud voice. I didn't like the feeling but did follow the order and fetched. I don't think that W L thought it cool to have a white friend he wasn't using in some way.

One evening W L and I were on the sidewalk in front of the new Breiding home. He had too many chemicals in his system to be rational. In his haze he sensed my fear and thought he heard insults and mistrust. He did hear fear and mistrust. He grabbed me by the jacket collar.

"Let's fight, cracker."

"There is no sense in me fighting you W L, we both know who'll win. If you want to fight, go ahead, but I'm not going to hit you back."

"You afraid to fight?"

"It would be useless for me to fight you W L. Anyway, you're my friend. I'm not going to hit you."

I was talking across W L's fist-full of my jacket jammed under my chin. I was strangely calm and resigned to whatever was going to happen. A few years later, white strip miners in West Virginia would scare me a whole lot worse.

W L pushed me up against a parked car and then back to the wall of the Breiding family's home. Back and forth W L pushed and jerked, trying to get me to swing at him.

Joan and her mother heard the commotion and came out to see what was going on. W L called Joan's mother a bitch. Joan ran down the steps after him, she shook her finger up in his face as he stumbled backward away from a four-foot-ten ninety-five-pound onslaught. "W. L. Sproul, how would you like it if I went up to your house and called your mother a bitch?"

W L retreated. He looked at Joan's mother. "I'm sorry, Mrs. Breiding, I should never call anyone's mother a bitch. I'm sorry, please, I'm sorry." W L was backing down the street, but even in genuine humility and chagrin his stumbling retreat had a swagger and the rhythmic clicks of the taps on his shoes.

That was the last time W L and I talked to one another. After that, W L just gave an embarrassed nod and said hello when we passed on the street. A friendship had been destroyed and W L realized what he had done.

I was confused and dismayed by this encounter with my friend. A couple of months earlier, W L had prevented an assault on the Breiding household that could have ended in robbery and murder. He showed up at the Breidings with two droopy eyed, mean-looking addicts. They wanted money for their habit. While W L sat with the after-dinner drummers and did his charming street hustle, the two wasted men stood, hiding behind sunglasses, one at each door leading out of the Breiding living room.

He just couldn't do it. He had become too close with the Breidings. The Breidings were from a place that sounded a lot like Mississippi to him— his people. He took his friends and left. Outside and a short way up the street, I think W L quarreled with them about going back in and robbing the Breiding family. It was a miracle of love that won out over the teeth grinding need for a fix. W L sent his two buddies away and came back inside and drummed.

I figured it was a blessing that W L was embarrassed about shoving me around. Neither of us would start over. We both understood that our worlds were too far apart and there were too many chemicals in between. I was glad W L had been my friend, and W L was my friend, or he wouldn't have felt embarrassment about shoving me around, and he wouldn't have called off the robbery.

After that, the Breidings and I had protection in the Fillmore district. I figure it was on W L's orders that his brothers never again hassled us. For a brief time, the Appalachian Scot-Irish mountain culture made friendly contact with ghetto Africa. It was just too complicated to continue.

Yosemite

At four-ten, Joan could walk under my outstretched arm. She was pretty, with beautiful, long, blond hair, and was built very well. We hitchhiked to Yosemite Valley with two huge backpacks of camping equipment, food and clothes.

In Mariposa, the Sheriff stopped and asked for identification. Joan was mistaken as a little girl so often that she carried her birth certificate. She showed it to the Sheriff, he looked at it and told us we weren't violating any law but that a woman had reported that there was a thirty-year old man and a ten-year old girl hitch-hiking. He suggested that we walk around a curve out of sight of the woman and hitch-hike there. We did that and finished our trip to Yosemite National Park.

As we walked into Yosemite, we saw a man stop his car, get out with the engine still running. He leaned on the open car door and took pictures, while his wife stayed in the car. After a minute or two, they joined the stream of traffic that, combined with the camp fires, created a haze of pollution throughout the beautiful valley—not the result that Yosemite explorer John Muir had hoped for.

Well-groomed tourists in coats, ties, and heels got off yellow and orange shuttle buses. Long limousines took rotund, well-dressed tourists from the lodge to some of nature's wildest scenes. Obese people struggled to get pictures of a bear that meandered unruffled.

A sign on the front of *Degnans*, a small grocery and supplies store, told us that personal conduct by every individual or group must be such as, "to give no offense to the majority of park visitors."

A barber shop and beauty salon had adjoining and elaborate rest rooms with hot water. One-eighth of the "salon" was liquor, 50% higher on most items, and 20 cent cokes when they were ten cents outside the park. (Yes, cokes were ten-cents in 1968.) They sold unripe avocados and firewood from cut-up fallen trees. There was a sign about proper dress, that without shirt or shoes there would be no service—it didn't mention pants. It reminded me of a rule at Washington and Lee

University that I heard about. Dinner jackets were required to be worn at dinner—there was no mention of pants, so the students showed up one day in dinner jackets and no pants.

If you dig people, whether they be straight or hip, here is a way to do it: Go to Yosemite Valley and pitch your tent in a straight camping area—you can distinguish straight from hip areas at a distance by the number of large campers parked in the area.

The straights take comforts of home to their camp ground—lawn chairs, radios, TV sets, canned food, table cloths, neat clothes and little flaming pots on poles to ward off mosquitos. They get dangerously close to bears with their cameras. In Yosemite, there was enough wealth in cameras and Coleman cookers to win President Johnson's War on Poverty.

They want to be friendly. Give them a chance, be nice to their kids, put their stuff away when it rains, tell them how to protect their food from bears. They get good vibes and become interested in you, loan you their axe (just bought for this trip), give you food and even invite you over for dinner. After dinner they talk, their fears are revealed, and their prejudices slip out.

If you are White, tell them of your good experiences with Blacks and your theories on why there are riots, etc., but give them plenty of time to talk. They'll learn from you and you from them. And one of them might be a cop from Sacramento, a young guy only two years on the force who thought Blacks were "funny people" who never sleep, call the cops then turn on them.

That cop thinks he is crazy for working eight hours a day, buying insurance, paying for a house, etc., when he could be in the wilderness fishing and living. And he doesn't think it's a policeman's job to put down student civil disobedience— "...how can police ever be looked to as someone who can help if they are seen with four-foot clubs beating people who don't have clubs?" He thinks it is a policeman's job to help people.

We were awakened by strange noises around the edge of our tent and a light flashing against the side of the tent. We were scared.

Finally, I got the nerve to look outside and saw bear cubs sniffing at the edge of our tent. They were most likely smelling for food that some campers had made the mistake of putting inside their tent with them. Our neighbor was directing his flashlight beams at the bears and the light was hitting our tent. The bears ran off and we tried to go back to sleep with adrenaline causing my heart to thump in my ears.

The air thinned as we climbed twenty-five hundred feet. Gravity pulled the less energetic molecules of oxygen into the valley floor. Our legs grew heavier as we climbed into the thinner air, we breathed harder and deeper. The lighthearted climb had become a trudge. We were slowed down to half-speed. It was the first time either of us had been so high—most of the mountain peaks back home in West Virginia are lower than the Yosemite Valley floor.

Yosemite Falls, a large shot of snow-melt water, blasted out over a cliff that had been gouged by an unimaginable ice mass inching its way under the steady influence of gravity.

From the valley floor the waterfall is a pencil-sized stream, but up close it is a roaring river, wider than Coal River back home in West Virginia and several feet deeper.

We climbed onto a piece of cliff that had, probably for many years, been slowly separating from the main wall. The railing at the edge of the cliff was made of one-inch water pipe. There was that skinny piece of pipe about chest high and then a twenty-five-hundred-foot drop!

I walked to the pipe, looked down, and staggered back. I was shaking, and my heart was thumping. On my knees, I crawled again to the edge and lay with my face out over the valley, looking down. A thrill went through my groin, up my spine and into my neck. On my stomach was the only way I could trust himself not to fall or jump.

It looked so scary and so innocent and so inviting. Maybe a person could glide down to the valley floor or hover like the hawk that was just twenty or so feet away. The hawk was unreal. It seemed to be floating on nothing. I want to come back as a hawk, I thought. I inched back from the edge, laid face-down on my crossed hands and shut my eyes.

Joan stood at the pipe, holding tight and smiling into the wind. She slowly looked down and then quickly up again. It's not easy to look straight down, so beautifully straight down.

Later, I imagined the struggle getting the pipe and the installation tools up through the thin air and wondered how long ago it was installed.

Taxi

The cab company hired anybody with a driver's license. There was no eyesight test, no driver training, and no criminal background check.

Cab driving was one of the lowest points in the economic hollow. The cabs were rattle-traps and they stunk. Mold from the upholstery burned my nostrils and made my eyes smart.

At shift change the cab station was a crossroads with every possible nationality, race, color, language, sexual orientation, and dress, mingled with the yellow of the rotting cabs.

Drivers claimed to be professors, writers, actors, poets, refugees, musicians, singers, and song writers. Some were revolutionaries whose armies were yet to materialize. Others were getting enough money together to finish their degree or to send home to Pakistan or Eritrea. Several never said what they were but looked and sounded like they were good friends with drugs and alcohol. Many were too close to forty to be so low in the pecking order. Men their age were running the country, teaching school, publishing books, raising kids, sleeping with soft lovers.

New drivers got the nightshift—midnight to eight in the morning. Endless messages squawked static from the dispatcher to all the drivers at the same time—it could not be turned off nor the volume turned down.

Almost eight hours into the first shift, with the radio torturing my coffee nerves and right at morning rush hour, I could no longer concentrate on what I was doing. My brain was full of mud with little bolts of lightning trying to get through. I ran a red light too long after it changed and got past the first lane, but the lead cars in the next two lanes knocked my cab into a parked car.

Through the mud and lightening came blue, yellow, and white flashing lights. No one was hurt. Everyone was glassy-eyed, nervous, and loud on caffeine. They had been driving in the going-to-work traffic, had maybe awakened grouchy and sure didn't need this. The fellow who owned the parked car was glad that his car got hit—he would get some money from the cab company.

I was amazed that I still had a job. The Teamsters Union was effective—my punishment was two days off at my convenience. I only wanted to work three days a week anyway. Which reminds me of the time President Jimmy Carter came to Charleston, West Virginia. He was a member of a panel discussing the National Energy Policy. Ed Smith, a coal miner for forty years, was on the panel. President Carter was cued to ask Mr. Smith why he only worked three days a week. "Because I can't get by on two," was Smith's answer.

The Zodiac Killer

"Shot him five times in the face." The news came from the driver at the next window.

"Who got shot five times in the face?" I was checking in with my fare list and money at the end of my second night as a cab driver. It was dawn and cold and gray. I was tired and felt the nerve tangled hollow alertness of caffeine.

"Cabbie got shot last night."

My first night was a wreck and the second was murder. Later that day, a man called from a phone booth in South San Francisco. He gave the San Francisco Chronicle details that only the killer could know. The next day a bloody piece of shirt tail came in the mail to the newspaper. The message with it included some symbols of the Zodiac that had been sent with previous taunts.

The "Zodiac Killer" had murdered several people. A few months earlier the killer thought he had finished off a picnicking couple, but the man lived and gave a description: Zodiac was an average looking slightly overweight White man.

I locked my cab doors and did not stop for lone White men. I ferried people in turbans and saris, any color, nationality, manner of dress, profession, sexual orientation, pimps, and prostitutes, but no lone White men.

One lone White man did get in my cab. I had parked in front of a bus terminal and went inside to use the toilet. When I got back to my cab there was a strange looking man in the back seat behind my driver's seat. I had forgot to lock my doors. I got in, looked back at my customer, pointed to the other side of the back seat and ordered him to move over—where I could see him. I was scared. His destination was in a dark isolated part of town. Yes, it was a relief when he paid and got out of the cab without killing me.

One night I got a big urge to urinate. I needed a rest room, but nowhere did I see a filling station that might have a public rest room. I was getting desperate to pee. I wanted to keep looking for a filling station and I didn't want to delay the search by stopping at red lights. Right turns were legal even when the traffic light was red. I turned right at every red light to keep looking for a place to pee. Finally, I couldn't hold it back any longer, I stopped the cab and ran into an alley and peed on a building wall.

After those first nights, I started thinking about getting out of that dangerous job. I figured this might have been how my uncle felt when he said to himself, on his first night in a coal mine, "If I get out of here alive, I will never come back."

Finocchios

In front of *Finocchios*, on Broadway Avenue, a woman waved one arm at my cab and held her drunken husband up with the other. When he could get his head up, the husband yelled something incoherent back over his shoulder in the direction of the club entrance—the saliva he tried to spit hung from his chin.

I slowly pulled up to the curb, reached back and unlocked the door. The woman tried to help her husband into the cab, but he pushed her arm away, hit his head and shin on the door and fell face-first into the moldy floor. She got him upright in the seat and pulled the door closed.

The drunk was a Los Angeles cop on vacation, with slobber running down his chin. He had just spit the devil out of his mouth. The sour smell of vomit drifted to my nose—I rolled my window down.

The cop's wife was trim, tall, neatly dressed, a handsome lady with a permanent look of worry. I figured she deserved better. She and her husband, whose weight-lifting muscles were covered with fat and whose belly had lost its discipline, were going just up the hill to the Fairmont Hotel.

"They ought to lock those people up, kill the scum, cock-suckers."

The wife winced.

"Jesus, what a bunch of perverts"

Back in Finocchios, the cop had taunted the chorus line. The gorgeous, lithe, long-legged dancers, were not women. One of the beautiful dancers plopped down on his lap and kissed him right on the mouth. Little did the cop know, but some of those men could kick his ass. At their day jobs, some were good looking men, weight lifters, body builders and one had been heard to say, "the only thing I like better than sucking cocks is kicking ass. I love a senseless fight."

"Jesus!" the cop spat on his foot and wiped at his mouth putting drool on the back of his hand which then touched his wife's dress. He looked at my long blond curly hair, kinked into a natural Afro, and went into a tirade against, "Long-haired-commie-faggots." No son of his better ever let his hair grow long and never, ever be a "goddamned hippy faggot protester."

The cop was going in and out of consciousness. There were sudden ten second blanks. He woke up and squinted his eyes to concentrate his vision. He belched and farted awful gases. I reached over and rolled down the window on the passenger side. Before he passed out, a second or two more of stupidity and incoherence worked its way from the cop's stammered brain.

It was easy for me to smile my way through the drunken tirade. The cop was so drunk that, short of pulling a gun, he was no threat. The wife apologized once more as they got out at the hotel and she tipped me more than the cab fare.

The cop threw up on the sidewalk. I was grateful it didn't go all over the back seat. Driving the rest of the night with the smell of vomit wouldn't be much fun. I drove back down to Broadway, looking for other visiting pilgrims.

Finocchios Chorus Line

Murder at the Cab Station

It was a beautiful November day, the prettiest time of the San Francisco year—a great day to be alive, to look at the sky and feel good about life. Suddenly we all let go of our gas nozzles, went silent and flat to the pavement.

The three pistol shots were instinctively recognized, even by those drivers who had never heard the retort of a small caliber pistol. Later some said it sounded a little like firecrackers, but not enough for anyone to risk staying in an upright target position.

Everybody laid low, especially one driver. He was on his back with his fare sheet clutched against his chest. He had a goatee like Patrice Lumumba and gazed, unblinking, at the sky. His eyes looked far away through the white clouds going slowly overhead that left patches of gorgeous, early November blue, San Francisco sky.

We slowly got up from behind our cabs and gathered around the dead driver. Flies were eating the blood that was already drying around the corner of the late driver's mouth. I remembered several summers ago, back home, when a twelve-year-old boy was hit by a car. There was a thud and the boy flew through the air. Flies got to his mouth in less time than it took me to jump a fence and get to the body. How do flies move that fast? How do they sense blood so well, so soon?

One driver edged closer, peered over the body, backed up and joined our circle of drivers—a circle about the size for playing drop the handkerchief at grade school recess. Nobody held anyone back, but no one went any closer, as if we all had hold of a giant hula hoop.

Subdued bits of exotic languages and strange versions of English were murmured. Ball caps, turbans, skull caps, head bands, dreadlocks, and all manner of cool gear, accented the faces that ranged from nearly no pigment to the black-purple of Gabon. The circle was united in one race, the race of the living. On the asphalt in the middle of the circle was someone who had no race.

When the police car drove up, we all backed off into a larger circle. The cops had been less than a hundred yards away from the murder, washing their cruiser in the cab facility, enjoying the sky and feeling glad to work in San Francisco.

The cop on the driver's side of the cruiser got out with a large, long-barreled pistol pointed to the same sky that the dead man was looking past. The passenger-side cop swung out with a shotgun. The dead man continued to stare at the sky, where a contrail was forming behind two hundred people headed for Hawaii.

The cops looked fearfully at the crowd for someone with a gun. They didn't know who they were looking for nor what the shooter looked like. There had been no description from the dispatcher. For all they knew, the killer could be standing in front of them with his gun still warm, ready to put a cop on the asphalt. They were big targets with their guns pointed to the blue sky.

Two cab drivers, in mirrored sunglasses and leather, gunned their motorcycles and sped away— one cop yelled stop, but they didn't. No one else made a move and the cops got braver and ordered the cab drivers back like they already were. We all moved back a step, which satisfied the cops.

The shooter had run away right after the killing. The day before, he had called the man he killed a friend. He knew him well, too well. Word went fast that the murder was over twenty dollars that the dead man owed the killer. One good thing about being dead is that you no longer owe anyone. Several drivers reckoned that there was more to it than money. It was not a good way to get twenty dollars back.

The nervous, confused shooter came back and gave himself up to the cops. It was better to have the cops catch him before the deceased's friends and relatives got their hands on him. Maybe it was better to come back and see if he really killed a man—there might be some way to backtrack and undo it.

The cops grabbed him, took the pistol out of his pocket and cuffed him roughly to make sure he knew who was boss and to let the crowd see how tough they could be—standard procedure learned at the police academy. The cops pushed the killer into the back seat of the cruiser. He was a small man, about fifty years old, a Grandpa.

The dead man was a dark handsome forty-year-old—in his recent life, a lean man with good muscle tone. Two little girls and their mother were waiting for him to come home from work.

The cops leaned against the open cruiser doors, fought against hyperventilation and reported in on the radio. They were soaked in sweat, trembling. Their hands shook as they tried to write their reports. Adrenaline, looking for something to do, roared through their systems. It would take a while to come down off one of the most powerful drugs on the streets of San Francisco. Until the adrenaline wore off they would compulsively tell the story over and over, shake their heads side to side and look far away.

A back-up cruiser arrived with blue lights and siren. The back-ups got out with their guns also pointed to the white clouds and blue sky. One had a sawed-off shotgun and worked the pump placing a shell into the chamber, intending fright for the circle of cab drivers. They left their cruiser doors open, motor running at a fast idle, and the blue lights flashing fear, confusion, and intimidation.

The ambulance, with red lights and siren at full blast, pulled up beside the dead cab driver. The flashy noise warned all bad-asses to back off. They loaded the debtor into the ambulance, left the lights flashing, siren screaming, and rushed a dead man to a hospital.

It was bad enough that the Zodiac Killer was out there waiting for me, but when I realized that my fellow cab drivers might be as crazy and dangerous, I quit. I just walked away, no notice, and headed up the street away from that place, forever. Driving a cab in San Francisco was not a job requiring a two week notice to quit. With no formalities, a cab driver just left or didn't show up when he got tired of driving.

My rattle-trap cab was still at the pumps, door open, and the gas hose nozzle hanging in the fill pipe. I talked out loud, as I hurried toward the downtown lights— "No wonder I only got two days off for wrecking a cab. Hell, I didn't murder anyone."

Gone Postal

Luckily for this unemployed cab driver, I got a notice in the mail that I had passed the test that landed me a job with the postal service. I went to work at SPO, a huge warehouse post office in South San Francisco, where letters and packages sent to soldiers across the Pacific were processed. I changed buses twice to get to my new job.

I learned that getting the mail out was not the top priority of the post office bosses at SPO. Their number one objective seemed to be to keep the workers under surveillance. Postal service supervisors spied through portholes from a hidden cat walk high above the swarm of workers.

I saw boxes, addressed to soldiers in Vietnam, thrown onto conveyor belts, where they sometimes busted apart. The cans of soup, tootsie rolls, socks, and homemade cookies meant for homesick boys overseas, were picked up and taped back into the busted box and sent on. But, when I absent mindedly leaned on a mail cart to get a little rest, I heard a yell from the supervisor whose main job seemed to be to stand and stare through a vodka haze at the workers and yell when they leaned on anything. That was their main job, to prevent leaning, not to make sure packages were carefully placed on the conveyor belts.

I got permission from my supervisor to go to the restroom. On the way, I stopped to talk with another worker. Immediately, I heard a whistle. I looked around and the supervisor waved and pointed in the direction of the rest room.

Some of the mail bags were marked with white chalk. I got a piece of the chalk and started adding peace symbols. I didn't care that I was being spied on through the portholes above.

My boss told me to help unload a tractor-trailer that was backed up to the outside dock. At first, three others and I were doing the job, then two of them were called off to another job. The remaining guy looked too soft to be a worker.

We talked as we finished unloading the truck. Our talk got around to the Vietnam War. The other guy told me that he had been a helicopter pilot there, and that they had painted a big peace sign on the bottom of their chopper. He asked me if those were my peace signs on all those mail bags. Before I realized that this might be a setup, I answered that they were mine.

On the bus to work my third night, I was reading a book. I looked out the window and thought I was near my stop. I pulled the string that rang a bell telling the driver to stop. I jumped out and looked around, nothing looked familiar, it wasn't my stop. I caught a bus going the other way and didn't go back to work at SPO for three months.

I started working for temporary agencies, moving boxes around and such. One temporary day, I drove a radio station van from their downtown studio to the transmission tower on the hill and delivered a manila envelope. It was a good job to help the hippies out—I picked up hitchhikers and shared their grass on our way through town.

Thanks to a bureaucratic oversight, I was hired by the post office to deliver door to door mail during the Christmas season. Prominent San Francisco politician Willie Brown lived on one of my routes.

After the Christmas substituting was over, I applied to be reinstated in my old job at SPO. To my surprise, I was reinstated to the post office job that I had walked away from three months earlier.

That reinstatement only lasted a month. The bosses weren't happy with my reinstatement. I guess I was fired for marking mail bags with peace signs and for leaning on mail hampers.

Lawrence Hall of Science

Teaching in the Peace Corps earned me an automatic California teaching license. That license gave me the opportunity to participate in a six-week workshop at the *Lawrence Hall of Science* in the hills above Berkeley, overlooking the San Francisco Bay.

In that workshop we learned by doing interesting hands-on activities for ninth grade science classes and constructed simple hands-on science equipment. After the six-weeks, we replaced science teachers and used our new knowledge and the equipment we had made. The replaced teachers were freed to attend the same six-week course.

The idea was to expose the students to hands-on activities for six weeks, get them used to it, and then bring back their teachers. Hopefully, student expectations would encourage the newly trained teachers to continue with hands-on activities.

I replaced a teacher at *Cabrillo School* in Pacifica. I observed his class before he started his six-week course at the *Lawrence Hall of Science.* He was not teaching anything when the Principal walked in. The teacher immediately went into a presentation on the metric system, something he had obviously prepared for surprise inspections.

Lawrence Hall of Science

Emeryville

After the Pacifica job, I substituted in Emeryville High School. Emeryville is a small town squeezed out of Oakland. Emeryville has always been industrial. When I was teaching at Emeryville High School, Shell Oil had a research center nearby—Emeryville is so small that everything is nearby.

The industrial tax base enabled Emeryville to build two world class schools, one high school, the other an elementary school. The high school had several playing fields, a bowling alley in the basement, a woodworking shop where the teacher taught students how to make and play guitars, and an atrium in the center of the school.

One day I was on playground duty when two boys got in a fight. With one in each hand, I took them to the office. On the way, the African-American boy called the White boy, "nigger." The White boy said, "The dude is color blind." The school was 80% African-American but bore no other similarity to a ghetto school.

Cambodia was invaded. The students wanted to march in protest to city hall and to the elementary school. They had to have a teacher with them. After being turned down by several of the full-time teachers, they asked me to march with them. I was given permission by the principal to do that.

As we walked along, on our way to the elementary school, we passed a re-built, pink Cadillac. One of the African-American students, whom I had become friends with, said something about a brother doing a fine job on his ride. I said that was racist—how did he know it belonged to a brother? He joked that white people shouldn't be allowed to own a pink Cadillac.

The elementary school students gathered in front of their school and listened to the high school students talk about Cambodia and the Vietnam war.

After the elementary school we marched to City Hall. No official came out to greet us. With a megaphone directed toward the City Hall, one of the students directed his message about Cambodia and the Vietnam war to the unresponsive building.

A student yelled "look," and pointed to an upstairs window where someone had a camera aimed right at me. I was never again called to substitute at Emeryville High School.

Hare Krishna

It was a perfect San Francisco Sunday for a fifty-two-block walk through Golden Gate Park to the Pacific Ocean along with an ungainly Krishna ship resembling a cobbled together third world construction project. Skinny, nearly bald Hare Krishnas, with little braided pigtails, hung all over the three-story bamboo scaffolding lashed to a wagon with large wooden wheels.

They chanted *Hare Rama Hare Krishna Rama Rama Krishna Krishna,* over and over and over. The words ran together like in the first grade when I messed with syllables until merged words became meaningless sounds. The last syllable of one word combined with the first syllable of the next and soon nothing made any sense.

Not making sense put the Hare Krishnas in ecstasy. If they ever thought of a reason for chanting, it was to slide out of reason and get high and lost on meaningless sounds. With silk wraps flowing, Hare Krishnas were a clutch of meditating, chanting, gone-crazy, easy free riders and free loaders.

Someone must stay in this world to make sure things get steered around the curves. god guided Krishna builders of this wonderful craft and god would do the steering. Specialists, sent by Krishna as expected, took charge of the steering.

Two fat ropes leading from the front served as a drive shaft. The brakes were two fat ropes trailing off the back of the creaky Krishna vessel.

Thousands joined the fun. Some took turns pulling the wagon, nudging it around the park's easy curves. Others were the brake—they held on to the back-end ropes to ease the ship down the park's gentle slopes.

Many of the folks in the parade were stoned on marijuana or LSD or speed or mushrooms or alcohol or love or delusions or the beautiful day or just *being,* and various combinations of it all. Krishnas were stoned on merged fronts and backs of words.

Indian music and drums and a mix of incense, patchouli oil, marijuana smoke, and eucalyptus drifted with the heady community joyously meandering through their beautiful park.

It was against policy, but some of the Krishnas were stoned out of their minds on more than chanting. I saw a friend we called Jimbo Freakout, a recent easy convert to lord Krishna. Jimbo hung by one arm from high on the scaffolding—he let his body swing around wherever gravity, acceleration and inertia wanted it to go.

I figured that unless Jimbo Freakout had a recent change in his habits, he was stoned on some illegal substance. Krishna didn't mind, he was just glad to have Mister Freakout aboard.

I found myself in a line of people, thirteen abreast. The celebrants got acquainted and passed marijuana joints down the line. The joints never ran out—the loaves and fishes, Krishna provides. We were amazed, stoned and amazed, that in a crowd of twenty thousand or so, everyone in that line of thirteen people were from West Virginia! Krishna works in mysterious ways. It was a miracle. Karma, man. It was god's presence. And why not, god always showed up at the Hare Krishna parade.

In that West Virginia brigade, I was with the Breiding family—two sisters and their four brothers and Mom. Mom was not stoned, and not bad looking for her age. This family made up eight of the fourteen West Virginians in that marching line.

A black Mercedes pulled to a stop on a cross street with the parade. A little saucer-eyed, sallow and sickly-looking man in a yellow silk robe, a beautiful necklace of flowers, and a red dot on his forehead, got out. He was freshly flown first class from India and driven to the parade in a rented Mercedes.

The chanters went berserk. They ran screaming to the incarnation of god on earth. The stoned, happy, and burnt-out cases prostrated themselves before the ugly and bored little god-person. They kissed his feet. Their undulating minds soared beyond time and matter. They laid face down before their god and left their bodies for what seemed to them to be several centuries.

The swami did a barefoot shuffle and chanted the mantra. Except for a coy, sheepish grin, the small man with the red dot on his forehead never changed his passive expression. I figured he must have done a lot of chanting to get that high, or someone had turned him on to some good drugs.

The Swami was a version of the lisping Ernest Angley, a television evangelist healer, who broadcast from Cuyahoga Falls, Ohio, to my Grandma back home in West Virginia. Ernest's toupee was always a little crooked, but he claimed that he cured AIDS with his touch.

The Pacific Ocean stopped the parade. Walking on water was not part of the program. The Krishna's miraculously fed everyone who wanted brown rice and beans. God provides loaves and fishes or improvises with brown rice and beans. It was Karma, man.

A few years later, when I returned home to West Virginia, I read in the *Charleston Gazette* that some of the Krishnas had moved to the northern panhandle of West Virginia. There they built a beautiful and luxurious grand gold palace financed by illegal sales of sports logo tee shirts, begging, and only lord Krishna knows what other mysterious income. They were prosecuted for the shirts. Their leader went to prison for molesting children and murder—the chant had quit working.

Palace of Gold at New Vrindaban, West

Virginia

Little god man.

ISKCON Founder-Acarya His Divine Grace A.C. Bhaktivedanta Swami Prabhupada

God-Man Two

Like Zachias, I was in a Golden Gate Park tree. A pretty woman looked up and we talked. She asked if I would like to meet god, in person, not die and meet god, but go meet a chain-smoking little Indian god. He smiled at everyone. His fifteen or so disciples said they believed that the little nicotine addict was god.

I guess they had rented the huge Methodist Cathedral and were holding what went like a business meeting of the faithful. A woman gave a report about a recent trip in which they took god out into the countryside. She reported that god admired his creation as he looked out the car window.

I lost track of the pretty woman who had lured me there. I looked around and she was gone, so I left.

Home Court

A girl friend and I were apartment sitting across the street from the panhandle of Golden Gate Park. For a few days, I went over to the basketball court. I loved basketball, some of the moves felt like I was a flying ballet dancer.

Men came to the court after work. They were always glad to see me and would toss me the ball for some warmup shoots. One day a new fellow showed up with an attitude about white people. He looked like he could back up the talk. He was about six feet tall and had the body of a man who lifts weights for definition. He could jump, he could shoot, and was better than anyone who played at the panhandle court. He pretended to ignore me and the other white man on the court. He boasted about how the brothers were excelling, and the brothers were the best.

Shooting foul shots determined teammates— the first four to make it were a team against the other four. The game went smoothly until it was tied at sixteen. I momentarily forgot where I was, what the ground rules were, and called a foul on the new man. The others looked surprised at me as I stepped out of bounds with the ball. What a mistake!

Back home in West Virginia, if you called a foul you got the ball out of bounds and players seldom questioned it. It was understood that if you called a foul, it wasn't a close call. I couldn't remember having arguments playing pickup basketball back home. But San Francisco was different. In San Francisco you didn't call fouls, you got even.

"Punk!" The new man yelled at me from just a few feet away. I knew that punk meant homosexual in street talk.

"I don't like being called a punk." I said back to him.

He leaped at me and hit me on both sides of my face at the same time and then a right cross followed by a left. I stumbled backwards, holding my face. Players grabbed New Feller, others grabbed me. Those holding me figured they didn't need to hold too tight, because I was out-matched. Without thinking it through, I pulled away from my handlers and hit New Feller one good time in the jaw.

I no longer considered the consequences, didn't care, I was over the edge, no more pushing, no running away. I had no idea what might be next. It didn't matter.

The whole world stopped and watched as I condensed all my past and future into one insignificant moment. Dying, life after death, heaven and hell, were meaningless concepts, there was only me and New Feller. I closed my eyes and jumped off the cliff, I was in free fall. It was a good day to die. New Feller could join me if he dared jump.

I went Kamikaze, with wild haymakers. It was all animal instinct now, and the next move was up to New Feller. Again, the other players separated us.

"Get on out of here, get out of here!" New Feller yelled at me.

I screamed that I would stay right where I was. "On this goddamn, fucking spot for as long as I want to, goddammit." I think my West Virginia accent came flooding out.

What New Feller heard, and saw, was a man who had nothing to lose, who wasn't kidding, who wasn't going to be bullied, wasn't going to leave without a bloody mess, and he didn't care whose blood it was. I was beyond caring, beyond thinking and reason.

I doubt if New Feller had ever seen nor heard a crazy Appalachian man, who was ready to die. He probably never heard the crazy voice of anyone prepared to die. New Feller didn't want to push it that far. He figured he could chase me off. He could whip me easily enough, but that wasn't what he wanted to have to do that day.

I was ready to fight until the end, not caring about the outcome. I was as crazy as an addled groundhog fighting dogs for survival. That can get messy. Not many people want to participate in that. As a pistol shot is not quite like a firecracker, New Feller did recognize the seriousness in my voice.

"Shit, this is crazy!" One player expressed the feeling of all the rest.

"Let's finish the game."

"You gonna play?" someone asked me.

It hadn't occurred to me that the game would continue. Nothing had occurred to me. I was planted and waiting for the world to act. I wasn't leaving.

"O.K., I'll play." I replied.

We were playing half court to twenty by twos, make it and take it. After a basket the scoring team got the ball out of bounds at mid-court. My team in-bounded the ball. The ball was stolen. New Feller had it and I guarded him. I fouled him and called it on myself, like we did back home.

"Well he is fair," New Feller said, I think trying to win favor with the men he wanted for brothers—I had out-maneuvered him on the public relations front.

The ball was thrown in to New Feller, he shot and missed, and I got the rebound. It was one-on-one with New Feller. I had more adrenaline in my system than he did. Normally, I am not a good jumper.

That adrenaline took me sky high. I jumped and shot with my hand inches above New Feller's outstretched hand. SWISH—the most beautiful sound in basketball. It was all net. The score was 18 to 16 and my team got possession of the ball. I had the ball again. I outjumped New Feller again. SWISH!

It was over. The score was twenty to sixteen. My team won!

New Feller walked off the court actually muttering, "I never lose, I never lose."

Everyone was fleeing the scene of the crime.

There would not be another game that day. The game to end all games had already been played. The tallest player on my team walked toward me on his way off the court and put a brown hand, palm down, on my white shoulder, and ran it the length of my arm and gave me five. I grinned like a possum eating sand briers, as I watched him and everyone else leave the park.

"Home court." I beamed.

The next day I *had* to go back to the court. If New Feller showed up and I wasn't there he would assume he had scared me off. He was there, watching the game in progress. I stood next to him and watched the game.

The first person who shows up after a game has already started forms a team to take on the winners. I turned to New Feller and asked, "Do you have the next game?" He ignored me. I asked again. He ignored me again. I stepped in front of him and repeated my question, "Do you have the next game?" He nodded his head yes, and I said, "I

CRV Committee of Returned Volunteers

I became the national vice-president of the Committee of Returned Volunteers. (CRV) That may sound bigger than it was. At a meeting of seven people, I voted for myself and the other nominee voted for me, it was four to three my favor.

Members of the Committee of Returned Volunteers were mainly veterans of the Peace Corps and members from similar organizations. Our purpose was to stop the Vietnam War. We turned out over one hundred members for anti-war demonstrations and rallies.

Joan Baez sang at one of those anti-war demonstrations, in the financial district of downtown San Francisco. Building windows were filled with admiring faces—I figure that they probably weren't anti-war as much as admirers of Baez. Baez was not the target of hate like Jane Fonda.

After one of her songs, John Kangas burned an American flag and his draft card. He was immediately arrested by plain clothes cops of some sort. Kangas was a returned Peace Corps volunteer. As vice-president of the Committee of Returned Volunteers, I gave a militant support speech, which I never followed through on (talk is cheap). John did two years in prison. He was the first person sentenced under the new flag burning law. I don't know why it surprised me but when he came out of prison his manner of speech was prison tough. Of course, after two years living with prison inmates, he talked like them.

Others of us placed our draft cards in a collection and they were sent to the Defense Department. Soon after that, my draft board contacted me and asked what my status was. At the time, I was a member of the inactive Air Force Reserves, so they couldn't draft me. Unlike the others, I had not risked anything by turning in my draft card. It took a while for it to occur to me that I may have influenced others to take a genuine risk while taking none myself.

Our San Francisco Bay Area Committee of Returned Volunteers had monthly meetings where we put a newsletter together and mailed it to our members. After the meetings, in the spirit of Emma Goldman[36], we partied.

I was the newsletter editor and when I decided to resign from that, I said that the next big issue was going to be the environment, because everyone, conservative or liberal, needs clean air and water.

---

[36] *She said, "A revolution without dancing is not a revolution worth having."*

Cuba

Americans were not allowed to travel to Cuba—not allowed by our government. In 1969, the Venceremos Brigade[37] was founded by members of the Students for a Democratic Society and Cuban officials. It was to show solidarity with the Cuban Revolution by working side by side with Cuban workers, challenging U.S. policies towards Cuba, including the United States embargo and travel ban. At the same time, our Committee of Returned Volunteers (CRV) arranged a trip to Cuba.

I answered a newspaper ad for a driver. With Joan Breiding, I drove a comfortable Buick from San Francisco to Houston. Joan flew back to San Francisco. A group of us CRV members flew to Mexico City and took a Cubana Airlines plane to Havana.

In the Mexico City airport, before we boarded the Cuban plane, we were directed by muscular men, whom I assumed were either police or intelligence agents, to get in a line where they took

---

[37] *http://www.venceremosbrigade.net/about.htm*

our individual pictures. I figured that our pictures would be shared with the CIA or FBI.

I was in Cuba when Neil Armstrong and "Buzz" Aldrin walked on the moon. It was July 20, 1969, a Sunday, and Aldrin took communion as he often did on Sundays back home where he was an elder in a Presbyterian church. NASA decided that the communion would have to be private and no mention of it broadcast back to earth—at this time NASA was fighting a lawsuit brought by Madalyn Murray O'Hair who had objected to the Apollo 8 crew reading from the book of Genesis. Her suit demanded that astronauts refrain from broadcasting religious activities while in space.

Aldrin chose to refrain from directly mentioning taking communion on the Moon. He described communion on the Moon in the October 1970 edition of *Guideposts* magazine and in his book *Return to Earth*.

Spare parts for specialized American-made equipment for sugar mills and other industries, were part of the trade embargo that the U.S. imposed on Cuba after the revolution. Lack of a $25 filter, made only in the U.S., could close a whole nickel plant. Rice that could have been bought from Louisiana was bought from China, at a much higher price because of the added transportation cost.

The trade embargo had hindered Cuba's imports of parts for repairing the island's fleet of General Motors buses. Cuba bought buses from the Soviet Union but was dissatisfied with the quality. They then bought buses from the British Leyland bus company. General Motors bought controlling interest in Leyland and prevented spare parts for bus repair from being sold to Cuba.

The trade embargo made it impossible to know if the Cuban experiment could work, too much of their resources were spent in increased transportation costs.

When I was in grade school, we lived in Ordnance Park in St. Albans. One of our neighbors married a Cuban and they were attending West Virginia State College. Her husband became a Methodist minister and they moved to Havana. He rose in Protestant rank to become president of the Cuban Council of Protestant Churches. I and two others of our CRV group visited them in their home.

She expressed dismay that her two children were members of the Young Pioneers which she saw as a communist organization. Her husband reminded her of the free medical care that they all got. He was not a member of the communist party, but he did take his turn as a gun carrying night time community guard.

Four of us CRV members went out walking one evening in a dock area. We met a man who had a car and needed some gasoline, we paid for his gas. He complained about the revolution. He said that before the revolution he could easily find a chicken to buy for food, but after the revolution there were none to be had.

We rode around with our new friend. He told us that the government had motels where a couple could rent a room by the hour and would get eight bottles of scarce beer. Two of us rented a room, we didn't use the room but did enjoy the beer.

We did some sugar cane cutting in the campaign to harvest one million tons for the year. We had lunch with workers from different occupations in a dining building. The workers, mostly women, were asked by their leaders for a show of hands by those who favored increasing their work day by an hour. They didn't get much response so had a second vote and by the third vote most of the tired looking workers held up their hands. I was surprised that they called for that vote in front of us CRV volunteers.

Cubans partied hard, danced and sang a lot, all of which I figure seemed puzzling to the inhibited Russian technicians. But sexually the Cubans were inhibited. I saw a woman get on a bus, the men turned and stared at her crouch—I suppose having sexual fantasies.

After the revolution Fidel Castro nor any living person could be shown on billboards. Images and references to Jose Marti[38] and Che Guevara were everywhere, but not Fidel Castro.

Jose Marti was a poet and revolutionary killed in 1885 leading rebels against the Spanish army in the fight for independence from Spain.

There was a popular young folk singer. He appealed to the idealism of his young fans by asking in his lyrics for the government to live up to the constitution and the ideals of Jose Marti, Che Guevara and Fidel Castro—a smart way to dissent in Cuba.

---

[38] *Jose Julian Marti Perez*

In the cities of third world countries, like Nigeria where I was in the Peace Corps, there were beggars everywhere in the cities. I saw only one beggar in Havana.

The Platt Amendment was passed by the U. S. Congress in 1901. It gave the U.S. the right to intervene for the protection of life, property and individual liberty. After the Spanish-American war occupation of 1898-1902, the Platt Amendment allowed for U.S. interventions in 1906, 1912 and 1917. The U.S. occupied Cuba from 1906 to 1909, and again 1917-1922.

In 1933 the U.S. and Cuban army put Sergeant Fulgencio Batista in power. Ironically, even as president of Cuba, he could not join the elite foreign dominated Yacht Club because he was a black man.

United Fruit owned parts of Cuba from the north shore to the south shore—to get from one end of Cuba to the other required passing through company check points.

In June 1960 oil refineries were nationalized because they wouldn't refine Soviet Union oil. Standard Oil, Shell, and Texaco let stocks of crude oil drop and sent their employee dependents home. It was claimed that they wanted to develop a serious shortage of oil and hope for a U.S. military intervention.

*****

One of our guides told of sitting with friends on a park bench to watch for missiles during the Russian missile crisis.

Back here in the U.S. Betty Boyd told me of her family planning to rendezvous at their isolated mountain property if a nuclear war started.

I was in the Peace Corps in Nigeria when Kennedy ordered our Navy to blockade Cuba and make Russian ships with missiles turn back and to inspect Russian ships leaving Cuba with the missiles.

In my idealism, I thought we were wrong to stop another country's ships on the high seas—turns out it was a *very* good idea to stop those ships. Castro had told Khrushchev that the Soviet Union should attack the U.S. with nuclear weapons if they invaded Cuba.

Nuclear war, which would have wiped out one-third of the world, did almost happen. Some of Kennedy's advisers wanted to wipe out the missiles in Cuba with an air attack.

Three of us helped unload a ship with bags of fish meal from Peru that could have been bought much nearer to Cuba. I almost got killed unloading those bags.

The bags were lowered on wooden pallets by crane from the ship and into a boat for delivery to shore. We removed them from the pallet, stacked them and moved out of the way.

After a while I got careless. The crane operator was alerted just in time, I looked up and saw a load of bags just inches above my head. We returned from Cuba on this ship after it was loaded with sugar for Canada.

Some members of the Weathermen, including Bernadine Dorn, were on our sugar boat to Canada. They ignored us CRV people. At first, I thought they were snobs.

Later, some of them blew themselves up while making a bomb in a Manhattan apartment, Maybe, they weren't talking to us to avoid a slip of the tongue that would give their plans away.

When I mentioned to one of them that my dad and grandfather had been coal miners, they warmed up to me. I had working class credentials—that is who they saw themselves working for.

Our sugar boat docked at St. Johns, New Brunswick. From St. Johns I hitched a ride with a man returning to New Hampshire from a fishing trip. We talked. I realized it was safe to tell him that I was returning from my illegal Cuba visit. We decided that we would tell the border guards that we were both fishing in Canada—it worked.

As I traveled south, people asked me if I was coming from Woodstock. At first, I didn't know what they were talking about. There had been no news in Cuba about the Woodstock gathering. I guess with my backpack and long hair, I looked the part.

When we got back in the U.S., I was told that everyone on the CRV Cuba trip but I was contacted by the FBI and interviewed. My friends joked that I changed addresses in San Francisco so often that even the FBI couldn't find me. It really didn't matter because I was not about to grant them an interview. I don't think I knew anything about Cuba that would have been new to the FBI. I was surprised that any of the others in our group did talk with the FBI.

Through the Freedom of Information Act, I found out that Aubrey Brown, one of the CRV

Cuba trip organizers, was questioned by an FBI agent posing as a newspaper reporter doing an article on CRV.

Cuban Revolutionaries

While in Cuba I wrote the following and it was included in the July-August, 1970, Bay Area Committee of Returned Volunteers newsletter:

Cuba is weird. It's hard to explain. Hard work is the motto. Too few people and too much to do. There is lots of work to do when you are the only country in the third world that gives every child under six a liter of milk per day, that employs everyone year round, that gives free medical care for everyone, that has free public phones and is abolishing rent, that is the only socialistic country in the western hemisphere that is plagued by a United States boycott that includes medicine and food.

We helped unload the ship that brought us back to North America. We unloaded the sacks of Peruvian fish meal that Cuba was forced by the U. S. boycott to buy in East Germany. There is much work to do when you spend so much of your money on transportation to get things in Europe that are produced next door in Latin America. Cuba would really be steaming if there were other revolutionary governments in Latin America to trade with.

But Uncle sugar and big business (spelled Imperialism) doesn't want revolutions in Latin America because to make things free or even available for the people will mean to take over American business interests. To American Imperialists these business interests are more important than milk for children, free health care, adequate diet, clean water and wages more than fifty cents a day that the Imperialists pay. (Attention all Imperialists: This is a ploy. I don't know the exact amount you pay your slaves but be cool and don't write an angry letter that will confirm what Mao said you guys do—pick up rocks to throw and drop them on your own feet.)

Imperialism is one word for saying things like big business profiteers.

I asked about the executions that occurred as the revolutionaries were consolidating power. The answer was that the "traitors" who were executed would have been attacked and killed in the streets by Cuban citizens if the government had not done it. I wonder if imprisonment was considered. Is there the possibility of due process in the wake of a revolution?

The Catholic church didn't allow separation of slave families, as a result, the Yoruba ethnic group of southern Nigeria are intact in Cuba with drumming, dancing, storytelling and the Santeria beliefs, all with Nigerian roots.

In the United States there was no continuity. African customs and language were dismembered. Slave family members were sold away from one another. Babies and children were ripped from their mothers and both sold. Adult married couples were separated and "sold down the river" sometimes to hot brutal labor in sugar cane plantations.

Fidel and Che

Defending America Against an Internal Enemy[39]

In late 1968, the Black Student Union and other student groups in the Third World Liberation Front did some research and documented what they could already see. The minority enrollment at San Francisco State College had been going down steadily for the past several years. It was becoming a white, middle class college.

On November 6, 1968, they called a student strike that lasted five months. At one time there were more than two thousand students and supporters in a marching picket line surrounding the small campus.

I watched the demonstrations with Randy Kehler, a friend who organized for the War Resisters League. We went in the College of Business to take a leak—exactly the wrong building. Tactical squad riot police headquarters was in the College of Business, of course it was.

Four tactical squad members followed us into the restroom. The first two cops jammed Randy

---

[39] *Some of this taken from http://www.sfsu.edu/news/2008/fall/8.html*

and me against the wall and demanded identification. The other two searched the stalls and wastebaskets.

I fumbled my driver's license and it fell to the floor.

"You dropped your card." The cop had a nasty curl to his lips. He didn't move back. I slid down and picked up the card with about six inches between me and the surly cop. One slight wrong move and I was going to get hurt. Randy had some granola in a bag, one cop looked inside the bag and then emptied it into the trash can.

In 1969, during the Vietnam War, Kehler returned his draft card to the Selective Service System. He refused to seek exemption as a conscientious objector, because he felt that was simply a form of cooperation with the US government's actions in Vietnam. After being called for induction and refusing to submit, he was charged with a federal crime. Found guilty at trial, Kehler served twenty-two months of a two-year sentence.

Daniel Ellsberg's exposure to Kehler in August 1969…was a pivotal event in Ellsberg's decision to copy and release the Pentagon Papers. It was Ellsberg's release of the Pentagon Papers which led President Nixon to create a group of in-

house spies, who undertook the ill-fated Watergate break-in, which led to Nixon's resignation.

The refusal of Randy and his wife Betsy Corner, since 1977, to pay taxes for military expenditures resulted in the 1989 Federal seizure and eventual legal forfeiture of their house in Colrain, Massachusetts. This was documented in the film An Act of Conscience (1997).[40]

Governor Ronald Reagan appointed S. I. Hayakawa as the new president of San Francisco State College, with orders to stop the demonstrations in whatever way necessary. The new president declared martial law and two hundred students were arrested.

Several strikers were seriously injured by four-foot wooden clubs, shaped like curved Samurai swords, coming down on their heads from the incensed mounted police. The police took the demonstration personally. They were defending America against an internal enemy.

Many San Francisco cops hated the dress, long hair, disdain for authority, and social mores of

[40]*https://en.wikipedia.org/wiki/Randy_Kehler*
http://nwtrcc.org/war-tax-resistance-resources/speakers-bureau/war-tax-resistance-speakers-bureau-randy-kehler/
[8]*http://www.sfsu.edu/news/2008/fall/8.html:*

the demonstrators. They especially hated the ones who chanted over and over to a hand clapped cadence, "It is time!" Clap, Clap. "To off the pigs!"

The cops could only stare with fuming disgust at what they saw as impudent, repulsive, un-American brats swaying to the beat of killing cops. The police were finally ordered to attack. Like Cossacks they chased the peasants, with swords held high and swinging low.

There were permanent head injuries that day, both physical and spiritual. These were mostly white youth being beaten by mostly white horsemen.

One of the cops threw up, another hyperventilated after the chase. Their bodies and emotions weren't nearly as tough as they tried to appear. Without the black boots and uniforms, many were beer-gutted with skinny legs.

Some cops liked the demonstrations—they got off on hurting people, and they liked the overtime pay.

From the 2008 fortieth anniversary of the San Francisco State College student strike.[41]

1968 student-led strike was the longest campus strike in United States history. The five-month event defined the University's core values of equity and social justice, laid the groundwork for establishment of the College of Ethnic Studies, and inspired the establishment of ethnic studies classes and programs at other universities throughout the country.

The Black Student Union and a coalition of other student groups known as the Third World Liberation Front (TWLF) led the strike, which began Nov. 6, 1968 and ended March 20, 1969. Clashes between the strikers and San Francisco Police tactical squads made national news. Students, faculty and community activists demanded equal access to public higher education, more senior faculty of color and a new curriculum that would embrace the history and culture of all people including ethnic minorities.

As a result, the College of Ethnic Studies was instituted in 1969 and hundreds of other higher education institutions across the country followed SF State's lead....

Many SF State strike alumni rose to prominence in the fields of social justice, law, public health, education and public service. They include actor and activist Danny Glover, who was

---

[41] *www.sfsu.edu/news/2008/fall/8.html*

a member of the Black Student Union, and Superior Court Judge Ronald Quidachay, who worked on the strike as a member of the Philippine American College Endeavor (PACE) and was a TWLF spokesperson. Alumnus and statesman Willie Brown, then a young lawyer and legislator, worked to free striking students who were jailed, as did former U.S. Congressman, Oakland Mayor and alumnus Ron Dellums.... Of the strikers who chose public education as a career, several returned to SF State and are currently on the faculty....

Random Sightings

There was no doubt who he was. When a man over seven feet tall looks like Wilt Chamberlain, that's him.

I walked between two parked cars at the San Francisco beach and there he was getting out of his car with two very large dogs. I decided not to say something awe-struck, I just said, "Nice dogs you got there." He said, "Thanks."

Another time, I saw Chamberlain riding his huge bicycle—imagine just how huge that bicycle had to be for a man over seven feet tall. He rode by where I was playing basketball on a Venice Beach court. It is not in any way connected, but I was playing for the first and probably only time in nothing but shoes, socks and bib overalls.

While I was shooting around at that same court, I saw a couple fucking on the grass lawn out in the middle of the park lawn, about one hundred feet away—when he finished, he got off and went for a walk, she laid there in post-coital satisfaction. I think I was the only one who saw them doing it.

Roosevelt Greer, a former all-American and all-Pro football player, was campaigning for Robert

Kennedy. He passed out Kennedy badges and bumper stickers there on Venice Beach and spoke to a group of us playing Volleyball. Greer was with Kennedy when he was murdered.

I don't remember where I met Bob Guitar nor his real name, but he did make an impression. He grew up in Ashville, North Carolina. He told me of going about the aircraft carrier he was on and painting huge peace signs on the bulkheads, while stoned on acid. Of course, he got caught. The Navy gave him a general discharge and a seventy-five-dollar monthly pension—in 1968 San Francisco that made him a rich hippie.

Bob had a beautiful blond guitar that he dearly loved and practiced on in all of his spare time, which was most of his time. He told me that on a bus, two young Black men said they were going to kick his ass if he didn't give them his guitar. Holding tight to his pride and joy he replied, "Then you better start kicking!" They didn't.

For a short time and a small rent, I shared my apartment in the Mission District with Bob. Once he disappeared for three days. Friends, who lived upstairs, said they too hadn't seen him for three days.

"Man, [he said man a lot], you can't guess where I've been." Bob said when he showed up on the fourth day of his absence. "I've been in jail, man."

"What for? I asked.

"For parking tickets, man! I went to jail for not paying parking tickets!"

Bob had invited a young woman from Mill Valley to fix Jewish food for his birthday, but he was in jail for the traffic tickets. I got the blintzes and got laid.

After Bob Guitar moved out, I contacted a switchboard in the Haight-Asbury area and told them I had a room to rent for $3 a night. Three young men from Chicago took the room. It cost them one dollar a day each to stay with me. They stayed for a few days and then disappeared with my TV and typewriter—the only things worth hocking.

They weren't very smart—one of them wrote to his girlfriend with my address as his return address. She wrote to him. I wrote back and told her what her boyfriend did.

After that robbery I was told that the local kids said they didn't rob me because I didn't have anything worth stealing.

The Breiding family placed an ad, at the Haight Street Free Clinic, about a room for rent. Another Bob showed up and took it. He was AWOL from the Army and that became his name, Bob AWOL.

AWOL was a motorcycle enthusiast and a good mechanic. He stripped out a Honda motorcycle engine and completely rebuilt it—all in the comfort of his bedroom in the basement of the Breiding home.

William, the youngest of the Breidings, told me that Bob kept the gas tank in his basement bedroom and huffed gasoline from it. William added that, "God knows how many brain cells he damaged doing that."

William said that, "I remember Bob AWOL most fondly, especially around food. Bob cooked all the time from the food he shoplifted. He used to make beans so hot, he would sweat profusely while eating them."

Bob needed a battery for the bike, so he stole one. He got caught in the act and the owner tried to chase him down. Surprisingly, for Bob was a chubby guy, he out-ran him. It was adrenaline, I suppose, and the fear of being picked up by the MPs.

Bob decided to go back to the Army. He turned himself in at the Presidio. The MPs punished him—they made him stand away from a wall and lean on the wall with only his two index fingers for support. That got painful, so after a while, when the guards weren't looking, he walked out the door and back to the Breiding home—AWOL again.

Bob got caught shoplifting a steak at the Lucky Supermarket at California and Mason (later Trader Joe's) —this led to his eventual return to the MPs, who didn't mistreat him this time. He did time in Fort Leavenworth where he learned the tailor's trade.

The bus driver called out "Please quit blocking the back exit." The woman in the exit well stood stiffly. From the back, I could see the two young Black men from the waist up. With fear on her face, she looked down at where her purse must have been, as the two young men robbed her. The men got off the bus and walked calmly up the street. The woman stumbled off the bus and walked awkwardly in the opposite direction.

I met a young man at a demonstration; he joined me for a cup of coffee. I mentioned forming a commune, he said, "Yeah, let's find some chicks and have a commune." His idea of a commune was about sex, I was immediately suspicious. I didn't, and none of my friends and allies ever referred to women as chicks. He went home with me to Bush Street.

I could tell he was uncomfortable with the lifestyle and dress of my friends at Bush Street. My suspicion grew. I told him I would walk him to the bus stop. When we went out the door a police car pulled up at the intersection a short distance up the street. The cop car flashed lights on and off a couple of times. I figured the flashing headlights might have been a signal. The guy might have been a young policeman from a neighboring town, put out as an undercover agent. I never saw him again.

Babs lived next door. I didn't wonder why a man was named or called Babs. In an anti-war march, I caught up with Babs and walked with him.

A line of men in front of us were dressed like women and doing the can-can. Then I saw it—their Gay Liberation Front banner. Of course, that's why he was called Babs, he was gay, duh!

When Huey Newton was convicted of voluntary manslaughter of an Oakland policeman, he was asked by an evening TV reporter if there would be violence or rioting in the streets over his conviction and prison sentence. He said that some of the "young warriors" might get violent.

The next day, as I walked, a small African-American boy, about twelve years old, came up and punched me one time in the belly, the little girl with him did the same. It didn't hurt—I saw it coming and had tightened my stomach muscles. They just walked away. That was it, the "young warriors" getting their bones, I guess.

Our Committee of Returned Volunteers had an office on Haight Street. After one of our meetings, someone asked me how I got back to where I lived on Bush Street. I told him that I just walk down Divisadero Street. He was surprised and said he wouldn't do that because Divisadero was all Black now. I hadn't even noticed. But that evening on my way home I did see that there were only Black people on the street. After that I too was afraid to walk down Divisadero street.

For a short time I lived on second avenue. There was a community organization that collected food orders every two weeks from the several households in the area and picked up fresh vegetables, eggs and cheese from a farmer's market in the Sacramento Valley. My order cost me about five dollars for a supply that easily lasted the two weeks. When the Forty-Niners played football at nearby Kezar Stadium, cars were moved out of driveways. To benefit the community organization we stood in front of our driveways and held up signs that said *Parking $10.* When we saw a luxury car approaching we turned our signs over— on the other side was *Parking $30.*

I was pleased to receive this quote from the West Virginia University *Summer Athenaeum*, July 24, 1969:

"The foreign student program reached its high point of effectiveness here after Julian Martin assumed the responsibility of foreign student coordinator in 1964. Under Martin, several programs and changes were launched to try to make the international student more a part of the campus and a less lonely and better adjusted student. One of these was International House on Willey Street, a place for foreign students to meet. For some years several of the students from abroad lived there. [International House was established by Dean Betty Boyd to give me an office and housing for a few foreign students.]

Another project was the Host Family Program, whereby Morgantown families "adopted" one or more foreign students and brought them into their households on frequent occasions. [Although I administered the Host Family Program. It too was started by Dean Betty Boyd.]

A host family in Preston County invited the new foreign students, at the beginning of the school years, to their Salem Church of the Brethren for a welcoming picnic provided by the church members. That host family stayed in touch with their student for years after he graduated.

The Carson Street Players

We sat around the kitchen table enjoying beer and marijuana. We had been getting together for a short time and the others didn't knew where I was from. I said something about a spiral notebook and pronounced it "spar ul." More than one said, "A what?" I said, "You know, it has a wire", which I pronounced "war," while I twirled my index finger to represent a wire on a spiral notebook. They asked, almost in unison, "Where are you from?"

Barbara, whose apartment it was, said, "How could you be so smart and be from West Virginia?" She was from the intellectually superior, Scarsdale, New York.

A group of aspiring actors had a grant to teach Shakespearian acting skills. We were to become the self-designated Carson Street Players. We met with them at a local grade school—and every time we were stoned on marijuana. We pretended that we didn't understand and would have to be coached to repeat things over and over. Finally, it got to our instructors and they informed us that because we were making no progress they were going to cancel the classes. We acted disappointed, probably better acting than we had previously demonstrated.

We went back to getting together, smoking dope and saying things that seemed cosmic and funny to us. Being stoned we laughed at anything. I thought it was funny to say to chubby Barbara, "Go down that chubby little hill and get us some ice cream."

Someone said, "I'm not paranoid, everybody else is." To which Sandy Weinstein replied, "Now it has been said in paranoid statements." Then Bruce said, "I think." While drinking beer and hard liquor, someone said, "Twenty million alcoholics couldn't be wrong." Hilarious stuff to stoned minds.

Not too far away was Don's Homemade Ice Cream shop. It was a hole in the wall that held about six people, with twenty or so in line outside. Thanks to marijuana munchies, Don prospered and opened stores in other parts of the Bay area.

Sandy Weinstein

When I met Sandy, he had dropped out as a stock broker in Pittsburgh and joined the hippie wars in San Francisco.

Except for Sandy, the Carson Street players split to the four corners. Sandy eventually visited me in rural West Virginia. But I haven't seen any of the others since those hilarious and munchy times.

Back home in West Virginia, I got this letter from Sandy (I didn't edit it):

"Constantly changing here—that's why I came here, why I stay and why I'll leave when I do. Sometimes it's incredible. In February we went to see Bob Dylan. Eleven of us—we rented a jitney bus, ate ½ ounce of grass in brownies, ½ tab of LSD and got dropped off at the door.

25,000 people dressed like it was a Thursday afternoon assembly in high school, ages 12-50. Dylan and the Band. Dylan in a three-piece black suit white shirt no tie the times they are a-changing. Dylan screaming all the lyrics ANGRY, VINDICTIVE, MOCKING like he just wrote the words. No record or concert ever sounded like this! He's doing a superstar thing right in front of everybody. The crowd is totally cued on how to behave by reading about every other night on the tour. Like a Rolling Stone is the last song and everybody knows it and knows they can surge forward. 10,000 crowd the stage. When he gets to the chorus he shrieks HOW DOES IT FEEL? 10,000 packed near the stage reach forward hands up. Everybody shrieks, the crowd goes beserk. More people yelling, running toward the stage, anticipating the next chorus...when you ain't got nothing to lose (but a three piece suit) you got nothing to lose (people running toward the stage) you're invisible, you got no secrets to conceal (crowd surges forward hands up toward HIM, he's yelling HOW DOES IT FEEL?

YAAAAAAAAAGH
IT FEELS GOOD
ITS MAGIC
ITS COSMIC
ITS SHOW BIZ FOLKS

It was great Julian...it was Dylan once a folksinger, once a poet—being a showman—always something people don't expect him to be but still on pure talent and EGO. EGO creating this THING in which 25,000 people felt the same surge at the same second. One of those momentary flashes in life when everything was one. Bullshit? I don't know. It blew out everyone who was there, nobody spoke at all on the ride home from OAKLAND. And he did it twice a night in 21 cities. Very weird.

209

Last nite we went to a movie house out near
Candlestick Park on San Bruno Ave. A live
Bluegrass group—it came from outer space, a 1953
movie in 3-D glasses and all and Flash Gordon
1935.

    an incredible barrage of experience and I
love it

             but
             sometimes
             I
             think
             of
             rain
             on
             a
             tin roof[42]

Have you noticed that the world has changed
slightly.
Welcome to the wonderful plentiful Post War Era.
Many people ask about you
What should I tell them

             Many many regards, Sandy.

Sandy went to India. His following unedited
letter is about that trip:

---

[42] *About his visit to our metal-roofed home near Griffithsville, West*
Virginia, on Sugar Tree Creek.

Dear Julian, Linda and Family

Back in San Francisco expecting to hear from you but i think its my turn to write ... I thought I'd be a prolific letter writer on my trip but i carried airgrams from town to town until the tropical humidity made them stick together...then id throw them out and look for another post office and so on...2 of 3 packages that I mailed home to my self never arrived and most letters sent to me never got to me. Well some trip. The ashram was amazing, beautiful, and extremely crazy...we held on for a long time (6 weeks) but swami's madness drove us away.... a man with extraordinary knowledge huge egomania non stop center of attention liar wife beater bad words to say about everyone much negativity and in the midst of the monsoon a lot of sickness. Thinking I went there to get well...we fled for our lives...me at 100 pounds...Sharon with hepatitis...not the total picture...much beauty and knowledge...including the well I already knew this but I have to do it myself......so I still can't fly...but if I want devote my life to it, I know how! Round 2...I know what I need to do...will I do it?

So, off we went on the 2 bit tour of India in which $3/day provides all we need at a level that dazzels Indians. We traveled by bus and trains down the coast of the Bay of Bengal to the southern tip where the bay meets the Indian ocean and the

Arabian sea and partially up the west coast finally living with an Indian family in a fishing village on the Arabian Sea in Kerala. Then we railroaded diagonally across the continent to Calcutta leaving India in January...it was incredible Julian...I've never been out of the country before before...what can I compare India too?...it turned out to be physically beautiful...and fascinating...lost in the past the way no other country seems to be. Indians are benign to a gentle extreme that gives contrast to our violent aggressive culture (surprising, right?). But really the extreme of it was a shock.

There is so much more to see there than what we did see that I'd love to go back...the drawback is that it is so extreme that it takes its toll...Staying healthy travelling in a tropical poor place seems impossible...we just adapt and hold on as best we could...and left not a moment too soon. Burned away by the intensity of life there...3-6 months seems to be the limit the mind and body can take in one dose...this letter sounds confusing...I loved it in India.

We continued east from India to Thailand beautiful beautiful country that we spent a month in and could have spent more time. Coming from India it seemed "western"...we went north to the golden triangle where the borders of Thailand, Burma and Laos, come together...went into the mountains where wandering tribes live...staying *with them in their villages and trekking around through their poppy fields…another amazing place that would have blown us away if we hadn't come from India…Hong Kong and home by mid-February…since then Sharon has been to New York to buy for her shop and yesterday left for Delaware to begin the summer. I'll be headed there too this summer what about you…the house we rent here is up for sale $160,000 our rent raised to $300/month before it's even sold…so we are to be out on the streets again soon…there is a rent freeze now for 60 days…too late…property has gone berserk here under the gun of asshole speculators…forgive me for not mentioning nuclear power, government and gasoline…I don't know where to direct my rage…so I'm working on other energies…*

Where and what are you these days???? Can you fly?????????

Love,
Sandy

Another unedited letter from Sandy:

Kite[43]
Tails
* of*

---

[43] *Roughly written on kite store letterhead with no, well, very little, editing*

*san
francisco
imported
kites
&
flying
paraphernalia
2253
union
street
583-5026*

*a lot of time in the last two years i thought about
writing or calling and i always set it aside...the
thoughts that are so good to write stoned drift away
whatever that means and so i just got your letter
but i'm stoned but if i set it aside ...and so......
....dear Julian how are you..i'm fine what's knew?
(fierce concentration a t this point to try to make
real sentences in a row.)   first, how would you like
a chronology of events (interspersed with things
you might like to hear about)*

*I had a little kite store for about a year and it
got to be a drag and all the kites were on boats and
there was a dock strike and then it was
Christmas...and in january not that many people
fly kites anyway and so one day we took all the
tables home and didn't go back sort of. but what*

you would have liked was that there was a whole
lot of things going   like a write up in Herb Caen[44]
and then a full page article in the sunday paper
called something like Wall st to kites ...and then a
film that was on the six oclock news and showed me
flying a kite and then an interview in the store ...
"is it a long way from wall st to here?.." until i was
forced to buy a Groucho Marx disguise. (I live
with cat...in a flat.. cat..catherine ! and i have been
together a yerar and a half... ... !!! we live with a
friend cathy ..and if have a dog and we live on 18th
sit at 4674A 18th 94114 and 863-6427 and 299-
34-8068. And then after the store closed i started
getting disabled welfare $239/month forever if i
don't work...sooner if i do.   And so we had a lot of
back payments so we drove to new york in four
days to see DeeDee off to Africa (linda just sent
a post card from Portugal where she is hanging out
with her sister and her parents and maya before
she goes,i think, back to Africa where shes been
since summer71 ?   Margaret[45] came back here
after being in Africa again and she is going to
school to be a nurse....) So when we got to new
York we were a little shaky about driving much and
when we got to Pittsburgh from where we hoped to

---

[44] *A popular column writer for the San Francisco Chronicle*
[45] *A former girlfriend in San Francisco*

hop on down my friends were in a dither (right, a dither) about just having a baby so we went to Cleveland after a day and so on...so bullshit you say but when we left san Francisco it was to go to west va ...well shit. (I ran into Clay downtown today... he told me he got married saturday and the room at firmont where they "spent the night" cost $120.) So x now i sit around a lot and grow things in the closet but there aren't that many people sitting around anymore,..and all those back payments so i bought a camera and i take a lot of pictures...yup that's cat...unhuh thats spot... and so on. with all of us racing through space so fast i don't know if it would seem the same to you but to me it seems a lot different here than maybe two years ago...remember all the energy tht used to buzz around carson st... the people who lived there are lots of different places and the energy isn't...where does it go to... where does what go? Its still san francisco here but as always san francisco compared to what.

Every postwar period in this country has been incredible haven't they. and so the war has been declared over this must be the post war period. think of the others...think of san francisco post ww2 and korea..whew the end of nostalgia and the striving for a new "modern" what will it be itll *leave the poor so far behind the country wont even hear their voices. does it seem like its going fast? ive never lived away from cities...are you away from these thoughts[46]...i feel in control of a lot of options...like leaving... "velcome to our country mr veinstein...papers please ($120?)   They have built a tower on top of twin peaks that is 1000 feet tall so tv reception will be improved ...at night.....it lights up. think how wide a tower has to be if it is 1000 feet tall.*

i feel peaceful a lot here...more than anywhere before but maybe because it is a city or maybe something else...changes keep right on coming...does being on land slow that down at least to the frequency of the seasons?

what could save this letter from rambling?...it would be nice to sit around and talk,julian and we will ..i'll get into driving a long way again or maybe youll do it. (Now and then thereS a gathering and it seems like all the accumulated changes are highly visible and so it always seems like a great time for you to show up...would you run out the front door ...please don't run out the front door. when you call carson st chimes ring!!! but the extension phones all have regular bells. But

---

[46] *Sandy had visited us on Sugar Tree Creek in Lincoln County, West Virginia.*

some days the clouds are so fluffy and blinding
white that everything seems very green and very
blue...almost sillouetted gainst a too bright daytime
sky and so the sunsets on days like that are very
purple and orange and all the houses in Oakland
look like theyre on fire..do you remember
hi anne[47]...were you at carson st last spring?
Julian ...i just read all this letter to this point and i
must tell you this... don't worry...on the other hand
dont show this letter to anyone who would measure
my sanity by it..im fine thanks...its just that i don't
write letters tha t f l o w...

        please please keep writing

    mythically

                     sandy
if you're really Julian, how come there's a stamp
on the envelope

A card from Sandy:

All this tinkering with science has destroyed
the planet starting with me. I am giving up my
exciting, tranquil carefree, sexy, devil may care,
envied rich and meaningful life in San Francisco.
Selling all my possesions including the ten year
Chinese packing crate foot stool and tie-dyed

---

[47] *I had told Sandy about new girlfriend Anne.*

218

shower curtain (former kitchen curtain, former living room curtain, former bed spread) and setting out for on one last venture into darkest Asia. If I can find the work that is alleged, I will try to stay for two years. Then back to US to find some place to work and live. I have burned out California and running against the economy. What next? If I knew now I would stay. Maybe I'll know then. Friends came close to buying farmland in West Virginia to get away but no. Sound fishy? I am are you?

Barbara Herzig

Not long after I left San Francisco for West Virginia, Barbara, of the Carson Street Players, wrote to me on the letter-head of the *Northeast Community Mental Health Services* of the San Francisco Department of Public Health:

August 7, 1973?
Dear Julian,
Do you like this stationary? I've been working for these people for 11 months now, and it's still ok   I haven't the faintest idea when I wrote you last or what I said, so if I repeat myself, just skip that part. First, my job. I now work 4 days a week, supposedly from 8 to 6 (10 hrs. a day, 4 days a week, = 40 hours) but I usually come in around 8:30 and leave at 5. The reason for these hours beside humanness, is that there is no work to do. We are in a community settlement house which houses a rec program, head start, and now a clinic open 8 hours a day, an extension of General Hospital services. If you don't know what I'm in, its community mental health, I'm the receptionist for 8 of us. Since the new clinic started, our space shortage became no space at all, and we have to tell people to come back because there is no room to talk. Besides which, there is no room for any

kind of day care, socialization stuff, which is
probably the most helpful thing for 90% of the
people who come to a clinic South of Market.
Talking isn't going to do much good for a chronic
nut who is first of all lonely. Knowing you, all this
talk might freak you out too, but I hope it doesn't.
So mostly now I just sit around all day long. I'd
really like to have some work, not piles that never
end, but some. The people I work with are super,
so that relieves some of the boredom since I can
talk to them without going crazy, for the most part.
The exception (The woman I share an office with is
a sixty-year-old Jewish lady[48] who tries to pretend
she is forty-five. She's at least as crazy as most of
the people who come in for help. Martyr,
complainer, smother-mother (she has a chronically
ill daughter, who is really chronically ill because
her mother made her that way. The two have a
neurotic set-up like I've never seen, and hope never
to see). Besides the people, hours are very flexible,
I go in and out as I please, and when there is work,
it is usually interesting. So, I'm still here and not
planning to quit for the near foreseeable future. It
really doesn't take much to satisfy me. Sometimes I
think it is good, sometimes I wonder about my lack
of ambition. Well fuck it all, it's been a good year.

---

[48] Barbara is Jewish, too.

Job aside, I've been going with the same person for very close to a year. I've never been that involved with a man before, I kind of dig it. Sometimes I get bored, but most of the time I enjoy the company, the security (it seems like a dirty word sometimes, but I'm finding it to be a very real need, I'm hardly as independent or liberated a woman as I would like to be) the closeness between us which only comes with time, is comfortable and comforting. The man is really just a kid still in lots of ways (he'll be 21 next month) and that freaks me occasionally, but a person is a person despite age, beauty, money, etc. I guess what I like is that he's really easy-going, and just accepts things as they are, here now. I'm exactly opposite, always planning, never really accepting things as they are. In fact, we're opposite in almost every possible way. I guess that's why we get along.

Oh, we just got a donation, a whole layer of a beautiful wedding cake. I plan to eat some right now. Delicious!

And now for the happenings around Carson St. Cat and Sandy have their own place now, bless them and us. Last winter, Sandy was so depressed. As you may know, when he's depressed, he's an absolute bastard to everyone around him. This was compounded by the fact that he and Jim did not get along at all. Jim and I lived together for about 4 months at Carson St. Even after he moved out, he *was over a lot. So, there was friction, something awful. When Sandy moved out, it was like a cloud was lifted from my life. Spot who was filthy and smelly, and noisy and gave off lots of negative vibes probably contributed a great deal to the feeling of an awful burden which hung around the place. Well, Cat and Sandy split three days after Deedee left for Africa via London. Waiting to move in for a month were Marian and Ricky (you remember him, he had the front room last Spring. Clay was also living there since January, again. So, the four of us live there for a while. Meanwhile Ricky was getting on everyone's nerves, incredibly. He couldn't find work, so he started taking a bunch of downers every day and was so obnoxious and messy and piggy. Also, he could never pay his bill. Whenever he had twenty dollars or so, he'd just go out and buy some more reds. We got more and more pissed off. Finally, Marian who has quite a well put together head on her shoulders threw him out. He still owes us like about $60 on phone bills, but he calls occasionally, promising to pay. Somedays I feel sorry for him, but now I am mostly mad at him. If there is anything at all worthwhile I've learned working with all the losers south of market, you get what you pay for, or, the winners win because that's how they get off, and the losers lose because that is the way they get off. I've seen too many people who say they want this or that get a chance* *to get it, and then blow it immediately. I've done it myself from time to time, we all do. But Ricky got his kicks off of feeling sorry for himself, and I got tired of playing into it, so screw him. So much for Ricky. Meanwhile the house is on sale. Rushlight wants $49,000 for it! That's really asking too much for a place as run down as 26 Carson. It's dirty and needs paint, and that you can attribute to having too many people living there for two years. And we did put a few holes in the walls, but the rest of the mess is Rushlight's cheap therefore sloppy repair work. We got new pipes because the old ones were completely clogged up from rusty years, and he didn't get anyone to finish plastering up the hole in the bathroom wall. We had to put a light switch on the wall in the john, and the workmen did such an awful job there is a hole in the wall. His brother and sister-in-law are selling the house. The brother is OK, but Bee is a bonnet, white glove bitch. Marian ran her out of the house last time she was showing it. Bee threatened to have dogs (there were three living there at the time) picked up by the pound, and Marian told her she'd have her picked up, too. We had such a great laugh when she was gone.*

Last week, Clay moved out too. He moved to a Morehouse in Oakland. I'm not sure what exactly they are about, more for the most part, especially more sex, and if you get it more money. I kind of miss him but life goes on. Sara finally went back to South Carolina, so Cocaine was living with us for a while. She is a great dog, so smart, and sexy. Clay, by the way is the world's biggest flirt. Every now and then he'd want to get it on with a chick somewhat seriously, but something would mess it up. Finally, I think he has met his match, a chick who hasn't fallen so in love with him that nothing is important. I'm glad for him, because, as far as I can tell, he really digs her. Anyway, our new roommate is a guy who is a friend of a friend of ours. He's gay, which is kind of weird, but he's nice, and no threat to me (I feel no need to compete with him or show my femininity with him). He's super heavy neurotic, but nice, and won't be too heavy a trip around the place, so I hope. I guess I am a little hesitant about living with a gay guy, but people are people, whatever their trip. And this in one city to get used to weird trips in. Besides Gerry, Clay's gay brother Tommy came out and stayed with us for about a month. He's a real nice guy and well put together and fun.

Well, that's all the news I think. My sister is canoeing down the Yukon River this summer, and I hope to go to Oregon for a week.

I heard you may come out in October for a week, would love to see you then, if not write, tell all, job? lovelife? Politics?

Take care, let us know what's up.

Love,
Barbara

PS Hope you didn't mind my typing, but it's easier than writing and the health clinic got 4 electric typewriters of which they use two in my office, after using a lousy manual for a year it's a trip to use it.

In the mid-nineties, I googled Barbara's phone number and asked about Sandy Weinstein. She said he had died seventeen years earlier of hepatitis that he got in his second trip to Asia.

Glide Memorial Methodist Church

Glide Memorial Methodist Church is in the Tenderloin district of San Francisco. It was just across the street from a Hilton Hotel, which accounts for Methodist tourists mistaking Glide for a church just like the one back home.

All the paraphernalia of the old church was gone. The communion alter-rails and the pews in the choir loft had been removed. There were carpeted steps leading up to the chancel area where the preacher's podium once stood. As the seats filled on a Sunday morning, people sat on the floor and on the carpeted steps that led up to the evacuated chancel area. All brands of folks, every color and hue, sexual preference, nationalities, tribes, cross dressers, all attended Glide.

Where the choir used to sing, a jazz combo played smooth comforting music. A long, dark-haired lady played flute and swayed with fecund sensuality. Vietnam War scenes flashed on the walls, as did Cesar Chavez, Martin Luther King, Jr., and Birmingham dogs. The gathering congregation looked up at banners and flags with spiritual and secular slogans, hanging from the walls. The flags swayed with the sexy flute player.

The combo faded out, the slide projectors were turned off. The walls returned to the colorful banners.

I had arrived late and was sitting on the carpeted second step that led up to the chancel area. The preacher strode and bounced to the center of the chancel area with a dazzling smile and yelled, "Good morning!" The audience returned the greeting, but not loud enough. The preacher repeated his greeting much like my drill instructor in boot camp. "I SAID Good Morning!" Half of the smiling, liberal congregation was happy to raise the roof with their response.

"That's better!" Replied Cecil Williams, the preacher, as he rocked up on his toes. The congregants smiled that Sunday morning good feeling smile, the smile that comes an hour or so before low blood sugar sets in and everybody, in the car on the way home, becomes irritable.

"Who traveled the farthest to be here today?" Williams called out.

Yells came back, such as Sri Lanka! Chile! Botswana!

Someone got close and aimed a camera at me. Then another, and then another. At least ten people took my picture. I thought that they must have thought that I was photogenic, good looking, or interesting, maybe.

Rev. Williams began an introduction of the guest speaker for the day. It was Jane Fonda and she was sitting right behind me and one step up— she was the good-looking photogenic aim of the cameras. Irritated with myself for being so vain, I snapped at the photographers to "leave her alone."

I met two women and got the phone number of the prettiest one and called her for a date. It was terrible, she ignored me for the three hours or so that I took her on a walk to places I enjoyed. I don't think she was interested in men. Another time more memorable, I arrived late at Glide and there were no empty seats.

I sat in the aisle next to a pew. When Rev. Williams asked who came the longest distance to be there, a pretty young woman leaned down and said close to my ear, "I'll bet there's no one else here from West Virginia."

"I'm from West Virginia." I said.

This was in a church! I did not waste the divine intervention, I went home with her.

Home Again

Grandpa Charlie Barker died. I decided to go home and stay with Grandma. She had never slept one night in a house by herself. Besides wanting to go back home to be with Grandma, San Francisco seemed to be getting more violent and I was starting to notice that the highway noise was constant, there was the Zodiac Killer, and people were being mugged within two blocks of where I lived.

A friend drove me across the Golden Gate Bridge up Route 101. In my navy field jacket, denim bellbottom jeans, army boots and what I called a toboggan, which the navy called a watch cap, I started hitchhiking home from the Mill Valley on-ramp. Beside me, on the berm of the road, I sat my old army surplus rucksack with an army goose feather and down sleeping bag tied on top.

The world was suddenly vast. I felt small and alone with my thumb out in the stream that flowed by my tiny spot in an expanding universe. I was spinning, revolving and falling at unknown speeds in infinite directions. The two times I got high on acid, I could feel all that movement, which being infinite, overwhelmed my circuits.

He drove onto the highway for a few miles, and if there weren't any male hitchhikers he circled back. He was meek, sat low down in the seat, spoke quietly, and just came right out with it almost as soon as I got in, "Would you like to have sex?" I silently shook my head no. Cruiser came to the northern end of his route, turned off the main road, let me out, and got back on the highway going the other direction.

When I was fifteen, a man cruising for sex in Ohio had picked me up. It was on my way back from the Indy 500. I was terrified of men "like that." Life in San Francisco mitigated that fear considerably.

A rusty VW van full of young, hairy people, pulled over and let me in. Inhaling the air in the van gave me a pleasant high. I joined the revelry and got royally stoned. Five miles later, I was at an on-ramp with my mind on Mars. The hairy ones hadn't given me a ride as much as a farewell party.

I had saved a hundred and fifty dollars that was folded and tucked into my watch pocket. It was a reserve for emergencies. I had twenty more dollars in my billfold. Except for the drug dealers among them, most hippies didn't have that much money. Up the road, some Hell's Angels would be recipients of about five of my dollars, a twelve-year-old hitchhiker would get some and Wisconsin state cops would relieve me of more.

North of Santa Rosa a wine salesman picked me up and said something about me being a hippie. I told him I was not a hippie.

"You see those people hitching there?"

I looked out the window and watched as we passed by a skinny bearded, longhaired man, colorfully clothed in beads and bellbottoms. His fat girlfriend sat on a big bundle of possessions smoking a cigarette. The skinny guy with his thumb out seemed in a hurry. The girl sitting on her bundle looked like it didn't matter to her if she ever got a ride. He was intense and nervous like a speed freak, but she had obviously been satisfied with something less electric, like junk food.

"They are hippies and that is what you look like. You may not consider yourself a hippie, but everybody else does."

"Except the real hippies." I insisted.

Near Eureka an organic farmer gave me a ride. He was a refugee from the San Francisco madness. As we talked, I asked the farmer what brought him to northern California. He answered, "Man it started getting crazy in the city. Bad vibes everywhere—the speed freaks took over Haight Street. In one year that street went from peace and love to a damned dangerous place. God, I hated to see those young girls being gobbled up by the vultures. They arrived there too late and thought those guys were the real thing. Some of them got into prostitution and hard drugs and diseases you wouldn't believe. Man, that's not why I went there.

My old lady and I got out and connected with back to the land freaks. We have completely cleaned up, don't even do marijuana anymore. We grow our own organic vegetables, built our own house, teach our kids at home. Want to join us?"

"Thanks man, but I've got to get back home to West Virginia. My Grandpa died, and my Grandma will be alone pretty soon if I don't get back. In her whole life she's never slept one night in a house by herself. There's always been family around."

When he got to his turn-off, the escapee stopped the car, we got out, shook hands and hugged. "Have a good life, man," we both said.

Hell's Angels

After some short rides, night fell near the Oregon border. I walked about ten feet into a dark wood, unrolled my sleeping bag and spent the night. I tried to forget about things like snakes and rats and whatever slimy mysterious northern California varmints and people-eaters might be lurking there. I fell straight asleep and what seemed like five minutes later, I opened my eyes and woke up to daylight and bird calls. I looked around and saw rusted cans—I had spent the night in an old trash dump.

I rolled up my sleeping bag, tied it on my backpack, pulled out my water bottle and answered the cry of my dry mouth. With some difficulty I overcame my piss hard-on and took a long welcome whiz. I shook it off, zipped up, cleaned my hands with dead leaves and stumbled out of the woods to gray overcast. I put my backpack down and before I put my thumb out, the first car stopped. I figured I was pretty lucky.

Dear baby Jesus! I was not as lucky as I thought. I was in a car with two Hell's Angels. The driver was handsome, dark haired and muscular.

His partner in the passenger seat was slinky and skinny with yellowed blond hair, an unhealthy complexion and a haunted look. The Angels were smoking pot to mellow down as they "kicked horse." They were going through heroin withdrawal and the dubbies were supposed to level the rough spots. But just to make sure, they swigged on some beer. In this whole world of cars, I drew these two outlaws. I looked out the window to take my mind off my new friends. They talked of their journey and pretty much ignored me.

I graciously accepted when slinky feller quietly handed a joint back to me. I didn't really want to get stoned, and especially with these two bandits. Recently, Mary Jane had made me a little paranoid and I had cut back on it. But I sure enough wasn't going to reject any offers of community from these guys. I had met fellows like them before. Sometimes the slightest thing triggered their distrust and paranoia into raging violence— like what had happened with W L Sproul. These two had heroin, marijuana, nicotine, and alcohol running all at once. I wondered what else might be in the mix.

I asked them where they were going. I knew

immediately that was dumb. Let sleeping dogs lie. If they don't talk to you, they probably won't form a bad opinion. But if you get to talking to them and they find out they don't like your sorry ass, or they detect fear, watch out. These guys were a serious form of crazy. It was not going to be a relaxing ride.

"We've got logging jobs waiting on us up in Oregon, working for the Bureau of Land Management. We have to show up clean, got to kick horse." The slinky blond looked at me out of the corner of his one un-squinted eye as he took a toke off the joint, held in the smoke with a grunt, and handed it to me again. The end of the joint was wet with spit. I closed my eyes and put the filthy thing to my lips. I rested my thumb on my lower lip, trying to avoid touching the spit, and sucked. This was good technique anyway—it made the smoke cooler by sucking in some air with it.

I opened my eyes to hand the joint to the driver and slinky man was still looking at me. I was in the wrong place with the wrong people, and everyone was stoned. The marijuana was making me anxious. I heard them talking about a prison life that wasn't very long ago. They talked of beating up protesting hippies at the Oakland military terminal.

"I sure got my rocks off kicking that hippie faggot son-of-a-bitch communist," slinky offered through the smoke.

Handsome feller added, "Far as I was concerned kicking those fucks was making love and not war. That was about as much as I loved them. If it had been war, I would have killed their sorry asses."

I thought I heard them say something about blowing someone away in a ditch. In my marijuana induced paranoia, I feared they were talking about me. Riding with these guys and smoking weed wasn't good.

They stopped at a little roadside diner. I eagerly paid for their cigarettes, coffee, and candy bars. Anything they wanted was okay with me. Now caffeine and sugar would mix with heroin, marijuana, nicotine and alcohol.

A plan was developing in my stoned mind. I waited until the very last second, until I saw the exit south of Eugene that would take me to Crowe Farm. "Here, right here, this exit here is where I get off. Stop!" I didn't want them to think about it. I wanted out of there before some irrational feeling gave them the idea to make me go with them and get blown away in some ditch up the road.

Handsome feller put on the breaks and pulled off the road. I opened the door just as the yellow haired slink turned around with a strange and what I thought was hostile look. But hostile was Slinky's only look. It was like my friend, Levi Harless, once told me, "Hell, Julian, it ain't you. They get out of bed looking like that."

That was the happiest exit from a car in my hitchhiking life. God, it was good to be alive and out of that car. I headed for Crowe Farm and purple faces, wild wolves, bleeding car grills and some crazy acid heads.

Crowe Farm

Crowe farm swarmed with stoned-out hippies and a few big, relatively sober men who ran things. Friends had recommended Crowe farm as a place where I might want to settle down. There was a craziness about Crowe farm, and anyway I had no plan to settle down until I got back to West Virginia and Grandma.

I was fresh meat. "Got any cigarettes?" was the first greeting from some of the inmates. Except for the big men, who were the obvious leaders, most of the rest were needy, dependent, unstable, desperate, broke and stoned or hung over. There wasn't any happy hippie magic.

The big fellows were afraid of narcs and a little suspicious of any newcomer. They checked me out with a car ride on the local back roads. We talked, drank beer, smoked weed, and they concluded that I wasn't a narc. When we got back, we played a little basketball. I made an impression with one of my shit shots. The big leader admired my hustle, and smarts. He hoped I would stick around.

I decided to stick around long enough to see

what happened on weekends. On Saturday afternoon people dropped acid and had visions and sightings. Things were changing colors. Some claimed to even smell colors. People got paranoid and feared others who gave off "bad vibes." One of the more troubled souls of the tribe played with some minds and told us that we had good reason to be paranoid.

Outside, the old junked cars were bleeding from the grills. I had gone out there to piss and saw the troubled soul coming toward me with an axe. I ducked back inside. The next day the cars had quit bleeding, there was an axe leaning against the wall near the door, and for Oregon the sun was bright.

I went on a wood cutting expedition. The Crowes had a contract to thin trees for the Bureau of Public Land. A carload of the big men headed out to the forest. One, who made no secret of being open to all forms of pleasure, told of trying to fuck one of the meek ones in the ass who was dog-fashion fucking his vegetarian girlfriend.

Feelings of Murder

I packed up my stuff and got the hell out of Crowe farm. I was disappointed—I had wanted the glorious idea of a commune to work. Crowe farm was worse than the regular world.

Years later I learned from a public radio reporter, who had visited communes all over the country, that most of those communes were not self-supporting—they were living off the money of the most recent converts. Core groups continued the communes; they welcomed new meat as the disillusioned moved on, sometimes with their life savings lost to the experiment.

A small Datsun stopped. The driver was about my age. He was going to eventually end up in Portland, but first he had to detour and make some deliveries over on the coast. West Virginia was a continent away, and the Oregon coast sounded interesting. I rationalized that Grandma was in good hands and would want me to enjoy my trip home.

The Datsun driver visited shops in small communities, showed his wares, and took orders for children's clothing. He was dressed for the job, he looked clean and pure with short sandy hair. We talked and talked and philosophized as only inexperienced young people can. At a warm and close moment, the salesman turned to me and said, "Do you ever have feelings like you want to kill someone?"

We were almost shoulder to shoulder in that small Datsun. All the alarms that thirty-three years can install in a person, went off. On the outside I seemed cool as freshly drawn well water, as cool as Fan Holler back home in West Virginia. Survival required that I look calm and conspire with every location in my brain that handled stuff like this. I looked at the salesman and said, "I think everybody has dark thoughts sometimes. I guess what we all must do is resist those thoughts. You are normal. Everybody gets feelings like that." I was anxious to reassure him and keep him calm. "We just have to put feelings like that away—push them out of our mind. Sometimes people feel those thoughts and see a doctor about what's going on. Sometimes they do that."

I was shaking my head up and down with pursed lips of certainty and hopes that I had not said the wrong thing—I didn't want to trigger him. "You probably don't need to see a doctor. You aren't letting those thoughts control you. You could read the bible and pray about it."

We didn't talk for a long time after that. I was sure this feller didn't mean that urge to kill when someone cuts him off on the highway. The children's clothing salesman was thinking some weird stuff.

When we got to Portland, the salesman invited me to his apartment to meet his wife.

"No thanks, I got to keep moving. But I appreciate the ride and it was nice talking with you."

I got out of the car and headed down the street to a Dairy Queen. I let out a sigh. I felt like I had been holding my breath ever since the murderous feelings came up. I inhaled deeply several times.

At the Dairy Queen, I got a chocolate milkshake, poured some coffee in it, and tried to calm down. I wondered if many people had murderous feelings and never said anything to anyone about them. Would that feller ever kill? Had he already killed? Were there any murdered hitchhikers found around these parts? Hell's Angels and a troubled children's clothing salesman was enough adventure.

I swallowed the last of the comforting chocolate coffee and got back to hitchhiking home. I made it all the way to Seattle and nary a ride was exciting, which was fine with me. The excitement started up again in Seattle.

From Seattle, I took the ferry to Orcas Island. On Orcas, I met seventy-five-year-old Johnny Jones who smoked pot. I encountered a colony of so-called hippies, who like elves, had built quaint, artistic, unheated and electricity-free huts that did repel rain and were different from anything I had ever seen.

Some good old boys on the island were giving the newcomers considerable grief. What they didn't know was that some of the strangers were excellent carpenters and had built kitchen cabinets for the sheriff. The 'elves' told the sheriff of their troubles. The sheriff stayed overnight in the colony and surprised the bullies with handcuffs and jail time.

I headed back to Seattle. At the ferry dock I met three people who were waiting for the ferry to

Seattle. We decided to get something to eat. We went across the road from the dock and climbed long wooden stairs up a small hill, to a bar and restaurant. We went in and sat down.

After an unusually long wait, a nervous waitress came to our booth. Holding tight to the menus, she said, "This is not a place to wait for the ferry. If you aren't going to order, please leave." The men at the bar looked around when they heard the waitress telling the strange looking longhairs to order or get out.

I said toward the bar, "See what happens in this country, just because of the way we look you all assume we are no good." Just then the biggest guy at the bar got up and grabbed me, pulled me out of my seat and started pushing me toward the side entrance. I tried to wiggle out of his clutches but was outside on the deck before the guy turned loose and held up his fists. Fear crossed his face, when he realized he was all alone with a crazy hippie. I punched him in the face. That ruckus brought reinforcements from the bar. Two of the alcohol emboldened men helped the big guy push me down the side deck and across the front deck toward the long wooden stairs.

At one point I had the leverage to throw one of the attackers over the deck banister, but understood it would escalate the situation, and passed up the opportunity. I lost my balance at the top of the steps and grabbed one of the brave ones by the shirt and took him down the first four or five steps. I tumbled to the ground at the bottom of the long stairs. When I got up, the men from the bar were still standing at the top looking down at me. I rubbed the knot on my head and massaged my arm that took the worst of it on the way down the steps.

I looked around and my three friends were gone, and the ferry was leaving. I called the sheriff, but he said he couldn't get there before the next ferry. It sounded like the sheriff really didn't want to enforce law and order on the local men at the bar, who were all old enough to vote. On the next ferry, I took a lonesome voyage back to Seattle.

Don's Orphanage

I had been waiting for about three hours in a coffee shop near the University of Washington campus and was feeling sad and lonely. I heard someone with a Bronx accent counting, "tree, four, five, six. Youse de guy dat needs da place ta stay?" I had put a note on the bulletin board by the door that read, "I need a place to crash. I am in the sixth booth behind you."

"Yes, I..." I started to answer.

"Come wid me." This fellow had two upper front teeth missing—a noticeable gap, thanks to Los Angeles cops who, he said, dumped him at the city limits and told him to never come back again. He wore a long, oversized, khaki coat in the style of Harpo Marx. I followed him. The chariot awaited in the form of an old rusted out Chrysler faded to a robin's egg blue body with a once white roof with huge tail fins that looked like they were welded on the previous year's model. It was in the image of my old clunker. Brand new, this yacht of the highways got ten miles a gallon.

In the car, I reached my hand to my benefactor. "Hi, my name is Julian."

The fellow said without turning his head or relaxing a two-handed grip on the steering wheel, "Day call me Spare Change, close de door soes we can go." Spare Change drove us to Don and Maria's, where Don was cooking dinner.

Don was a short, stout man with blond hair and the stiff muscles of a weightlifter—they made him look like he was getting ready to flap his arms. He was a plasterer by trade and a Marine veteran. His wife, Maria, was the daughter of a farm worker family from Mexico. The oldest of their five children was only eight. Maria had her hands full. They lived with several shipwrecked souls in a lonely single-family house with warehouses nearby.

Don ran an adult orphanage for people he picked up off the street. Anyone was welcome to stay as long as they wanted. Some had been with him for almost a year. He was their counselor, their confessor, their benefactor, their hefe. Don was Robin Hood.

Smells from the kitchen were like home cooking with Mexican spices. My stomach signaled that it was past time to eat. Don fed spaghetti with jalapeno peppers and chunks of steak all through it to seven people besides his wife and five kids. After dinner they all chipped in and washed the dishes. Don got out his guitar and played and sang everything from Mexican ballads to the Beatles to country music.

Don's merry band took me to a large grocery store. The routine was for everyone to go in a different direction and try to pull attention away from Spare Change, who would put meat into the big inside pockets of his Harpo Marx coat.

Spare Change stole for about a minute and then started putting cheaper food in his cart. The manager suspected he had shoplifters on his hands, but before he could figure it out, Spare Change looked like any other shopper, except for the distinguished coat, strolling the aisles putting items "innocently" in his cart. The Harpo coat hung heavy with meat. When Spare Change accelerated it didn't stand back with its usual flourish.

We took the food back to the orphanage, and marinated the meat, for future meals to feed weary, homeless, travelers. Every now and then Don made Spare Change wash his coat of many shopliftings. Besides no front teeth, Spare Change apparently had no olfactory nerves.

The community association members were discussing how to spend their federal grant when Don and his happy social workers entered. Don's tall, white cowboy hat was punched up round in the top. He looked taller than his five-foot-five.

The community association had officers and a paid director. Don tore the meeting up by arguing that they should just take the grant money and divide it evenly among all the residents in the community. The director opposed it, he probably didn't like having nothing to do and maybe no salary.

Don quoted scripture, "If thou wilt be perfect, go and sell what thou hast, and give to the poor, and thou shalt have treasure in Heaven."

It made the rich young bureaucrat unhappy.

Don stood up and pointed at the officers and director who were sitting behind a table in the front of the room and said, "You people just want the money for yourselves!" The merry band stood when Don stood. Don stood and pointed, and they stood and pointed, they were equals.

The stone-faced director responded, "It is a better use of the resources to pool the money and finance a project that will benefit the community. The community gets no benefit if the money is dribbled away here and there."

"Yeah, like your salary isn't dribbling money away." Don was stabbing his finger at the director. His disciples were stabbing their fingers and saying, "yeah!" following Don's lead.

Don lectured, "Let's take your $18,000 salary and put every household's address in a hat and draw eighteen addresses and give them each one thousand dollars. That could pay some people's rent for ten months. Let's divide up your expense account the same way. Or maybe you could take everyone out to dinner instead of those stuffed shirts you usually treat to free meals. Let's do the same thing with the money you are paid for plane trips to D. C."

"Money for meals and travel expenses are in a separate account. It can only be spent for those designated purposes," the director replied.

"You are lying!" Don shouted.

Spare Change, who didn't have a clue about high finance but could recognize a phony from far off, yelled, "Yeah!"

"You are out of order sir!" The director yelled

at Don through the howl and din of the merry band.

The meeting disintegrated. Everybody was talking at the same time. The place was in an uproar. Don was an idea man. He didn't hang around to see how they implemented his proposals. His disciples followed him out the door. Don smiled with satisfaction. The troops laughed as they patted him on the back. Don knew he should be humble in victory, but he did swagger a little.

"Way da go Don. You sure told dem cock suckers." Spare Change observed. Don only tolerated cursing away from the house and Maria and the kids.

"Took de words right outta my mouth, Don," Spare Change continued as his empty, blood stained, Harpo coat caught the breeze and blew back from his waist. He looked like he was going to take off flying. It would be Spare Change as superman, smelling like dead meat.

We piled into the Chrysler and headed back to the castle. It was a royal chariot with the Roman centurions riding home from another victory over the Visigoths.

Five skinny, scared, and weak looking young

men, whose clothing announced that they were pretending to be some variety of Hell's Angels, showed up at Don's orphanage. Long knives hung from their belts. They wore berets and headbands. "Devil's Kin" blazed across the backs of their vests and leather jackets. Their black boots had knife pockets. There were leather chaps, stainless steel chains swinging to their wallets, iron crosses hanging from necklaces, and arms with menacing swastika tattoos.

Don welcomed the "Devil's Kin." The merry band cooked up a big meal. The faux devils never said thank you, nor did they help with the dishes. The sleaziest of the bunch looked at Maria. Don caught his eye, and without saying a word let him know that he would be one sorry biker if he didn't keep his eyes off her.

Don gave the Devils a big room upstairs. The brave bikers stacked furniture against the door before they went to sleep. I figured that Don didn't have any reason to be afraid of these guys unless he turned his back on them or gave them cause to become a mob. One on one, they were scared— maybe fear was why they traveled in a band and pretended to be mean. Don said later that they needed love that they must have lived lives without love and didn't trust anyone to be kind to them. Don believed everyone should get what they need. But they need not need Maria.

I left Don's orphanage and headed north on a bus. The Canadian border police took a look and escorted me off the bus and searched everything I had. They even made me empty all my money. The obese border policeman, who seemed to be permanently pasted to his chair, put all the bills in the same direction and ordered them from lowest to highest with president heads up.

He handed me the money and said, "You should always keep your money like this." I dropped it and picked it up in no special order and stuck the wadded bills into my pocket. "God is random, mister border policeman." I winked at the pained look on the helpful money shuffler's face and headed for the bus.

Vancouver

Ah Vancouver. I had never been in a place where snow-covered mountains looked like they were just two blocks over. Vancouver was peace and hippies were everywhere. Canadians weren't in the Vietnam War, and they were not concerned about the cosmic meaning of long hair. Vancouver people didn't care about appearance. Wear what you want. It was San Francisco minus the mean cops.

I looked up Heather, a woman I had met in Golden Gate Park. In San Francisco, she had been company for a Japanese businessman, who was busy trading in the financial district. She invited me to stay with her if I ever got to Vancouver. In Vancouver, we made love—no, we fucked, it was not love.

Heather had a huge dog and lived in a house of gay men. I didn't get a good look at her in San Francisco. In Seattle, she looked tired and sad. It dawned on me that she was probably part of an escort service, maybe a call girl. I ran away.

In the evening, I went for a walk along the beach. I sat down on a log and enjoyed the twilight sky and the good feeling of being in a place far away from anything I was used to.

"Good evening," a tall, thin man said as he sat down on my log. After we traded small talk, the man suddenly stood up, took a couple of steps and turned around. He stared at my crotch as we continued talking. I got the point, smiled and said, "No, I'm not interested." The man saluted from the brim of his hat and said, "Enjoy your evening." He continued down the beach.

The next morning, I saw the man of the night before walking just ahead of me. How strange it seemed that probably no one else around the man, approaching him on the sidewalk or seeing him cross the street, had any idea that last night he was searching for another male body to make him feel better. Had they known, it wouldn't have mattered. Vancouver was that kind of place.

I wondered, as I looked at other people walking the streets, just what they had done last night. What secret, lusty thing went on with these people going so seriously to work? I imagined making fuck with the women I saw.

I headed to Stanley Park to get my backpack that I had hid under a bush where I had spent the night. In the park, near Lost Lagoon pond, I met Grace who was probably forty years older. We walked around the park together. She had read about Canadian young people heading for Vancouver and wanted to find out what was going on. She had boarded a bus in Toronto and arrived in Vancouver the evening before. It was like being with Grandma. She was talkative and fun to thump around with. We went to the edge of the park and bought a city map. A Vancouver motorcycle cop approached.

"What are you looking for?"

"The Panda Restaurant," I motioned down to the map that Grace and I were studying.

The cop gave us directions, smiled, and eased down the street. I watched him pull away. No San Francisco cop had ever been that friendly. Canada wasn't at war.

We went to the next corner and stuck our thumbs out in the direction the cop said to go. An old Dodge convertible pulled over and we got in with three students from Bellingham College. They too were looking for the Panda restaurant. Grace and I had the map out when the sound of a motorcycle approached. We turned and saw the same cop balancing on his chopper with a big smile on his face.

"Still looking for the Panda? Follow me." He took off, with his lights flashing, and went down a one-way alley the wrong way and stopped in front of the Panda. We followed him and parked near the Panda. A small curious crowd watched as we talked with the friendly cop on the hog.

As the cop pulled away, I said, "They could sure use you in San Francisco."

"But they aren't going to get me." He smiled and waved good-bye.

After a big Chinese lunch, the students took me to their campus just across the border. My eyes had turned to the plump college girl. She let me sleep with her, but no sex. I was frustrated, and sleepless when I got back to Vancouver.

I went over to Heather's to say goodbye. One thing led to another and she gave me the clap. While I was off with the college girl, Heather had had a reunion with her bisexual boyfriend. When she found out her boyfriend was infected she took me to a clinic.

I think Heather knew she would never see this country boy again. I was the second West Virginia lover to pass her way—the other was an African American sailor from Morgantown.

Heather drove me to the outskirts of town. I started hitchhiking across Canada.

Get in Friend

I had my backpack, sleeping bag, money in
my pocket, and a bottle of antibiotic pills. With my
thumb out, I was on my way across Canada. It was
a slow start. It took two hours to get a ride out of
Vancouver. I took a piss by the side of the road,
and as the urine splashed on the gravel, my dick
burned.

I wondered what had happened to Grace.
Damn! When we got with the younger people, I
forgot all about her. I remember her saying she felt
like a fifth wheel. She wasn't in the car when we
left the Panda. I wondered if she was all right and
felt guilty for forgetting about her. She was a nice
lady, and I ended up ignoring her for a piece of ass
that didn't happen.

Except for a burning penis when I pissed, my
body was humming—I felt weightless, free, happy
and rested. Waiting for me in Saskatchewan, there
were antelope mixed with cows out in a pasture
that the road bisected. And some Wisconsin State
Police patrolled an interstate highway and had
nothing better to do than harass hitchhikers.

Route One goes north for a while and then turns southeast. At the turn, another road continues north with a sign pointing toward the Yukon—it looked barren.

Young Indians yelled something with a mocking sound as they drove past, giving me the bird out the windows. Indians? I hadn't ciphered them in. I figured there were some crazies out on the road looking to do something irrationally satisfying. I had not factored in hostile Indians.

Near dark, an old white Cadillac stopped. The driver reached over and opened the front door for me. An only slightly healthier dark-haired version of the sleazy, horse-kicking Hell's Angel, greeted me with, "Get in friend." He was heading for Calgary, coming back from his monthly masturbation with chance in Las Vegas. I had no idea there were people addicted enough to drive thirteen hundred miles to gamble. I threw my pack in the back seat and got in.

"Thanks very much for stopping."

"Where you going, friend?" The driver said with a lopsided smirk. He was skinny and weak looking. He was unaware of the smirk, it was his best presentation, and he meant it for a smile. He was too small for the big car, kind of lost in the seat, like Spare Change in the chariot.

"All the way to Emmons."

"Where is that?"

"West Virginia."

"Gee, I've got an aunt who lives in Roanoke," he said with tobacco stained teeth showing through the smirk.

"Roanoke is in Virginia. I'm going to West Virginia." It didn't do any good, the feller referred to my home country as "Virginie" the rest of the ride. I wondered if people in the Dakotas and the Carolinas have the same problem. Hell, I had learned in the eighth grade the names of all fifty states, their capitals, and where they were on the map.

I thought I saw gentleness in my host— someone who wanted to help. I also suspected that if I returned smile for smile it could lead to something else between us. I was not sure just what, but there was invitation in the driver's smile. Maybe it was just invitation to friendship from a lonely gambling man.

Every ride that comes to a hitchhiker brings a touch of warning. Is the driver sane? Is this safe?

Picking up hitchhikers can be dangerous, too—hitchhikers in Montana ate the guy. They didn't eat all of him but that probably didn't seem like a difference to the victim.

When the cannibals got to California and came down from LSD, they turned themselves in to the police. "Here's his thumb," convinced the doubting police that those two innocent looking teenagers were telling the truth.

I was relieved when my new friend stopped to pick up another hitchhiker. A young man with blond curly hair, who could have passed for my brother, got in the back seat. The driver was cleared now—he wasn't an axe murderer, or he wouldn't be driving with two hitchhikers, with one sitting right behind him.

I and the other hitchhiker wanted to see the Rockies in the daylight, but our driver was going to drive through them in the dark. In Banff National Park, he took us up a dark gravel road to a big picnic shelter and said goodbye with his innocent smirk. Warm in down sleeping bags, we slept that cold, damp night on picnic tables under the shelter.

I awoke at dawn and wanted to travel alone. I quietly rolled up my sleeping bag, tied it on my pack, and left the other hitchhiker sleeping.
I sat down on the tail end of my army surplus poncho in the gravel by the side of the road. I stuck my thumb up in the misty drizzle.

I would have been satisfied to sit there for a long time, looking up at the Rocky Mountains through the occasional break in the mist. I was there, instead of Calgary, just to see those mountains.

No hurry, a ride would eventually come along. Right then was all that mattered. No worries for tomorrow and no regrets about yesterday, although, taking a piss reminded me to regret last week. But it was getting better. The pills were working. Years later, I was glad that it was not years later that I met Heather, or I might have had AIDS instead of the clap.

Technocracy

A Canadian family looked out on the wet road and saw a bearded young man sitting on the gravel looking from under an army poncho, with his thumb poked up into the misty rain. They didn't look away and pass him by—Good Samaritans for sure. They did their Christian duty and gave me a ride.

The Creed family didn't seem to be afraid that I was going to eat them. The mother did take the precaution of giving her front seat to me and moving to the back seat with her thirteen-year-old daughter. When I spoke to her, the girl blushed and smiled across her braces.

They had never met anyone from West Virginia, but they did know it wasn't Virginia. When they stopped for gas, I went to pee. It still burned. Damn! I was riding with these nice people and had the clap. I washed my hands well.

We drove straight through Banff—an eyesore of gaudy shops waiting for suckers. Outside town, I saw a family of goats licking the pavement. After generations of licking the road, goats probably couldn't find natural salt. Wild now included licking the asphalt. I thought of Fort Indians, whose wildness was reduced to expecting handouts from the Army.

Bill Creed believed that people with the education and ability to manage a country should run governments. He called it technocracy. I didn't rain on the parade by bringing up Robert McNamara, the master technocrat.

In Bill Creed's system, McNamara clones would run the government. After what those clones did to Vietnam, I wondered what they would do if they were all turned loose again with their calculators.[49] They would probably calculate a way to eliminate people and run the nation efficiently. McNamara later confessed that we emotional, low-tech, anti-war protesters, were right about the war all along.

The Creeds were as good as they seemed. They were steady, intelligent, hardworking farmers who practiced their Christian beliefs—the salt of the earth. I rode all day with them through the Rockies and into the red-hot town of Moosejaw

---

[49] *Years later, the "shock and awe" destruction of Iraq answered that question.*

where the Creeds were staying the night with relatives.

Bill Creed, Mary and their daughter Lou Ann all got out of the car and shook my well-washed hand and wished me safe journey. They headed back down the road to spend the night with Bill's brother.

A road sign stood above my outstretched thumb. Cars occasionally and slowly came out onto the highway, passed by me and turned into a city street within eyesight. It was a slow day. Few cars were traveling out of Moosejaw. I looked closer at the road sign and saw scribbled messages— "I was here two days, Jeff Pellegrini, June 5, 1961," … "36 hours September 12, 1963, Randy White." The sign was full of scratched warnings to the traveler.

I was having no better luck than my predecessors. It was about two hours until dark. I walked down the road and checked out the underside of a bridge for a possible night's lodging. The smell of piss pushed me away.

Back at the sign, another kind Canadian stopped and told me how hard it was to get a ride in that spot. I pointed at the warnings on the sign. The Canadian laughed, he hadn't seen the messages before. "There's a youth hostel two miles back. Maybe you could hook up with a ride there or spend the night. It only costs fifty cents." It sounded a lot better than the bridge.

"Thank you very much. I'll try this spot until it gets close to dark and then go down there if I can't get a ride. Thanks a lot. I appreciate it very much."

I stood awhile in the loneliness of a hitchhiker in Moosejaw and started walking toward a bed and away from the sign and stinking bridge.

The hostel was four trailers parked in a square. One trailer housed the caretaker and her office. "That'll be fifty cents, and there will be coffee and donuts here in the morning."

The government of Canada set up hostels across the country for the thousands of young people on their odysseys. I thought that this sure was a civilized idea—different from the States. Hell, they killed young, White antiwar demonstrators at Kent State and young African-Americans at Jackson State, and they beat the hell out of the peacemakers at the Democratic Party convention.

The Canadians seemed to cherish their kids. Many Americans wanted their kids to get a haircut, a job, and die for their country. Canadians didn't see long hair and outrageous dress as the sign of a traitor—they weren't in a war which seemed to require that in the States. Fifty cents a night!

A van load of Americans came in the youth hostel office while I was signing up, and they too were amazed, and grateful. One of them kept saying, "Out of sight, man." Their looks gave me an uneasy feeling, reminding me of the big fellows at Crowe farm.

Their name was Creed and they were staying with Bill's brother. The very first Creed in the Moosejaw phone book was the right one. I called it and said, "Hello. Is there a Bill Creed visiting you all?"

"This is Bill." He answered.

I explained my situation and asked if I could ride with them the next day.

"You bet. How about if we pick you up at eight o'clock in the morning, at the hostel?"

"Mr. Creed, thank you very much, I really appreciate this."

I took my first shower since leaving Vancouver and slept well that night. I dreamed of home.

It rained the second day I rode with the Good Samaritan family. We talked and talked until the Creeds had to turn south. They stopped and treated me to a farewell dinner. I promised to write when I got home. Two days of sharing stories and theories had made us friends. Mary Creed cried as I got out into the rain.

Tears welled in my eyes as I said, "It has been a wonderful two days, thank you very much for your kindness. I don't know how I can repay you."

"Just remember to pass it on to someone else," Bill Creed answered. I thought of the clap. Lou Ann smiled shyly.

Here, Martin, is our address. Please write us when you get safely home.

"Take care of yourself, Martin." Mary said through her tears as they pulled away and headed south toward home.

Winnipeg

Somebody in Wisconsin knew I had that money in my watch pocket. They were waiting for me in a squad car. But I would keep them waiting a little longer.

I was in the middle of nowhere, watching antelope across the road graze with the cows. I felt like I had taken a most wonderful drug. It must have been something I ate or didn't eat. No cares, a beautiful blue sky with some just-right white clouds, Jesus rays ready for the final call, antelope, cows, the blissful solitude and my penis not burning quite as badly. Maybe I was having that nice day everyone in San Francisco had wished me.

A car stopped, I joined a good seminarian who already had two hitchhikers. We spent the rest of the day getting to Winnipeg. We talked the talk of young vagabonds, of sports, politics, sex, philosophy, and we talked of religion.

I mentioned that it would be good to spend this Christmas at home. The others nodded agreement except for Joe, from Quebec. He said that Christmas was a farce, that they can't possibly know when Jesus was born or when he was

278

murdered, that there is no historical record and it isn't in the Bible.

Jesus was murdered? I had never thought of it as murder, or that he was killed. In my mind he had always been crucified. But, yeah, it was murder.

Joe said, "How about torture and assassination?"

"Man, that too." I said out loud.

Joe was on a roll. "Think about what happens around Christmas. The days quit getting shorter and start getting longer. The so-called pagans celebrated the hope of more sunshine. The "pagans" must have had a name for their spiritual beliefs other than a name that means primitive heathens—not something nice to call yourself.

The Christians were just recently pagans, so they continued to celebrate the winter solstice, the winter sun stop. For the sun to head back in the direction it came, it would obviously have to stop. And they tucked the little baby Jesus right in there."

"But why is Christmas on the twenty fifth? Isn't the shortest day of the year a couple of days before that?" I asked the swarthy pagan.

"Well I think that the Christian bosses offered the twenty-fifth as a counter celebration, kind of like the Soviet Union substituted a New Year celebration for Christmas. Or maybe the pagans waited a few days after the shortest day of the year to make sure it was really happening—to make sure there was still hope. Maybe the twenty-fifth was their day too.

They probably partied for a week or two, and the exact day didn't matter too much. They had no way of knowing for sure that the days weren't just going to keep on getting shorter and shorter until all they had was darkness."

Man! Was my most consistent remark.

"When they decided that they were going to be saved from the shortening days, then my friend, they threw a party. They had big feasts, invited all their friends, ate pigs and ate like pigs, got drunker than hoot owls, beat drums like crazy, danced to a frenzy and fucked their brains out."

I glanced at the seminarian who peered straight ahead—no reaction. There was a slight arc of a grin on his face. He added, "Also, by the 25th they knew the sun was coming back because at noon, it was a noticeably one degree above the southern horizon."

"The Christians stole it. It fit right in. Jesus was a message of hope, the days getting longer was a message of hope. Jesus was saving people from Hell, from burning alive forever in a lake of fire. The sun was saving people from eternal darkness and freezing their asses off. And buddy, don't you think that maybe Santa Claus was a preparation for Jesus? You get little kids to believe in someone who rewards them if they are good and they slide right on into the Jesus myth as adults."

Here, dear reader, I pause for a poem written by my late friend Ivan Hunter. Ivan, for thirty years, was the poetic postmaster in Nitro, West Virginia:

The first day must have been a wonder
Nobody knew what came next or how
long it was to last.
Everybody cried at sunset the first time
And waited up all night to see if day was
coming back
                 Ivan Norton Hunter

The conversation cycle reached magic moments when everyone was silent for a spell. And it was a spell. Talking stopped. No one was uncomfortable with it. It just happened with no planning. It felt good and right for the moment. It was like light waves canceling one another and the result being darkness or sound waves out of phase opposing other sound waves, creating what passes for silence. Any attempt at conversation rushed into the rarefaction and was dampened to less than a whisper. It was like a quiet time in the woods.

A boy of twelve was hitchhiking alone. The good seminarian had four hitchhikers now. When we stopped for lunch, the boy tried to steal the tip the seminarian left. With his empty pockets and no home, the boy didn't think twice—the money was there unattended. Don't get caught was his guiding principle and survival his main joy. I took him back to the table and made him put the money down. The boy giggled—he liked the attention.

My Back Room

I lay on a royal catafalque in the middle of an underground stream that wound through a grotto. I laid in state on satins and furs and struggled to rise to the surface. I gasped for breath and sat up. Another hitchhiker was snoring in the dark basement. I felt like I had been holding my breath for an hour. I was spent. It was sleep apnea.

If you never woke up, it could get strange in those dream caves. No matter how educated, smart, or worldly wise, everybody has an amazing dream world, one that can disturb, fascinate, puzzle and scare the hell out of a genius or an idiot. People are random equals when it comes to the dream world. Of course, not everyone can dream up the benzene ring.[50]

After a real breakfast, the seminarian's mother handed each hitchhiker a bag with sandwiches, an apple and some homemade cookies. Everybody promised to write. The twelve-year-old and I were dropped off at an intersection of two highways. I was heading south toward Minneapolis. The boy was going in a forlorn

---

[50]*August Kekule's dream of a snake swallowing its tail.*

easterly direction. I worried for my little brother. The boy would have gladly gone home with me. I pained for him, but wasn't prepared to sell all I had, give it to the poor and follow Jesus. I handed the kid five dollars. "Take care of yourself, little buddy."

I got into my ride out of Winnipeg, looked through the side window and waved goodbye. The boy, lighting a cigarette, looked up just in time to grin and give a little wave.

I pushed the boy into the back room in my mind and shut the door. Sometimes the folks inside that room force the door open and wander out. Skippy was in there. Tiny Skippy had died trying to give birth to pups belonging to a neighbor's huge dog. She pushed her insides out. A ground squirrel lived in that room—I had shot it with a 410 shotgun and watched it die as it pumped blood up thorough a small shot hole. Some slaughtered hogs and cattle were there, a tough guinea hen, A chicken or two with wrung necks, all kinds of snakes, and the stuttering boy I bullied in grade school. The Zodiac killer, was in there too. I shut the door to my secret room and stuck my thumb out.

Country Roads

"Country road, take me home to the place I belong, West Virginia…" John Denver's voice came out as I opened the car door of a "switchboard" volunteer.[51]

It was one of those cosmic coincidences that bring credence to the idea that there is a god, who just breaks in every now and then and does something quirky, akin to reversing gravity. It was a sign, I wondered if god was looking out for me on top of not believing in gods.

"That's where I'm going." I ducked into the back seat. "I've never heard that song before, that's where I'm going! I can't believe this is happening." I looked at the other people in the car to see if they understood. They were smiling. They all nodded and grinned. "It's your karma, man. You're being called home. Here, have a toke," spoke one of the marijuana-wizened heads as he handed me the lit joint. I took a drag, held it in and passed it back. I didn't go for that karma stuff. It wasn't his karma

---

[51] *Minneapolis, like San Francisco, had "switchboards" where travelers got help finding a place to crash for the night. A private version of what the Canadian government was doing for its meandering children.*

that put out dad's eye in a coal mine accident—it was fear of poverty, coal company greed and gravity.

I had been on the road when *Country Roads* started its worldwide journey. Years later, in Munich, I heard it from street musicians. And when I told an internet technician in India that I was calling from West Virginia he said, "Country Roads." My daughter Bess, sung it in a youth camp in California. When John Denver sung it at a West Virginia anniversary celebration, teenagers started dancing and chanting, "We're number one, we're number one." We are on the bottom in so many polls that we take any first place we can get, with embarrassing pride. It was obvious that *Country Roads* was about western Virginia—the Blue Ridge Mountains and the Shenandoah River are mostly in Virginia and in West Virginia for only five miles. *In the Blueridge Mountains of Virginia* is the first line in the song, *The Trail of the Lonesome Pine*

Chicago and Home

Big legs and hips squeezed me from both sides. I was in the back seat, between two large state cop trainees. The cops took me to a post office to mail in the $80 fine. My offense was hitchhiking on the interstate.

"Of all the crimes being committed out there, why are you all wasting time on me. You ought to be chasing the real criminals," I said from the back seat in the canyon between the giants.

"You broke the law, and you are going to pay for it." The driver answered.

I talked to them about what was happening to the world, to the environment. "In fifty years this whole world is going to collapse if we don't stop destroying everything."

"In fifty years we will be too old or too dead for it to matter," the biggest trainee said, without turning to look at me.

"Don't you care about your grandchildren?" I said looking at the trainee. He ignored me and pointed out the window to the exit sign they were looking for and informed the driver. They pulled off the interstate and into a small town and drove to the post office. I walked inside escorted by the big cops—their guns were cannons, leather was black and heavy and shiny, uniforms clean and pressed, brass polished, black shoes like mirrors. I made out an eighty-dollar money order payable to the proper authority and mailed it with my ticket to the county courthouse.

Back in the car I asked, "Were you all at the demonstrations in Madison? I saw that on TV in San Francisco, I was cheering for the other side." I said.

"Hell, we were too. The more they demonstrated the more overtime we got." One of the cops said.

They let me out at the bottom of an interstate on-ramp.

"You can hitchhike from here, but don't get back on the interstate or we will put you in jail." I just looked at them and muttered motherfuckers under my breath. The police probably knew approximately what I was muttering. They drove off laughing.

I went up on a bridge that crossed the interstate and stuck my thumb in the air. A driver looked up, got off at the next exit, circled back and gave me a ride to Chicago.

I had an address in Chicago of three ex-Peace Corps nurses who ran the Committee of Returned Volunteers Chicago office. The medicine worked, my dick wasn't burning anymore. Chicago was a nice stop. One of the nurses and I kissed passionately. The roommate who stayed up the latest did the wild thing with me.

I spent some of my remaining dollars on a bus ticket and slept from Chicago to Cincinnati. Standing by the road, with my thumb out, east of Cincinnati, I smelled the moist, dense, fertile Appalachian Mountains. I took deep satisfying breaths. Home was coming out to meet me and egg me on, come on home boy, come on home, it's still here.[52]

---

[52] *When I got to Grandma's, I wrote to the Creeds to tell them that I had made it safely home and to thank them again.*

Made in the USA
Middletown, DE
18 January 2019